An Assembly for Wales

Senedd i Gymru

Contents

Executive
Summary

Introduction

Proposals for a Welsh Assembly go back 100 years. The last Labour government legislated for an Assembly in the Wales Act 1978, but it was rejected by four to one in a referendum in 1979. Labour, the Liberal Democrats and Plaid Cymru still support the creation of an Assembly. The Conservatives remain opposed, but have introduced further administrative devolution to Wales. Labour's proposed Assembly would have executive powers, and be elected by first past the post. The Liberal Democrats and Plaid Cymru both propose a Senedd with law making powers, to be elected by proportional representation.

Public opinion surveys in Wales suggest some 45% are in favour of an Assembly with 30% against and 25% don't knows. Of the 70% in favour and undecided, 50% want an Assembly with limited legislative and revenue raising power, 60% want proportional representation, and 70% want a referendum on the issue.

Lessons from the 1970s

The Wales Act 1978 proposed an Assembly with executive power only. It set out a complex scheme of legislation which gave no clear picture of what powers were being devolved. It would have created an uneven patchwork of devolved powers, varying with the degree of discretion conferred by existing statutes, none drafted with devolution in mind. It might not have created a stable settlement.

Devolution in the 1990s

The major change is the much greater impact of Europe; and the reorganisation of Welsh local government into a single tier of 22 unitary authorities. From the policy statements of the opposition parties the main objectives for an Assembly appear to be:
- to make the Welsh Office and quangos more directly accountable.
- to reflect the distinctive needs and cultural identity of Wales.
- to remedy the democratic deficit which led to the introduction of the poll tax and changes in education and the health service which had no support in Wales.
- to give Wales a strong and distinctive voice in Europe.
- to provide the new unitary authorities with strategic direction and support.

Role and Functions of an Assembly

The classic functions of a democratic assembly are making laws; controlling government expenditure and taxation; and providing democratic scrutiny. The Liberal Democrats and Plaid Cymru both propose a Senedd with law making powers. Labour's Assembly would have powers to pass secondary legislation, which would vary with the degree of discretion conferred by statutes passed at Westminster. Most Westminster legislation applies to England and Wales.

If the Assembly is to develop (or preserve) separate policies for Wales in local government, education or the health service it will need legislative powers. Otherwise it will be dependent on the legislation passed at Westminster and prepared by Whitehall, where the government may have a different agenda and other priorities.

The Assembly should also be able to call Welsh political leaders to account more frequently and effectively than does Westminster.

Powers of an Assembly

Executive Devolution

If the policy is one of **executive devolution** this could be achieved by
- listing in detail all the powers transferred, as in the Wales Act 1978, which would take a lot of time to negotiate in Whitehall; or
- transferring all the executive powers exercisable by the Secretary of State for Wales, without itemising them.

Labour have proposed that an executive Assembly should have **limited legislative power** to restructure quangos and local government and to legislate on the Welsh language. The Assembly could legislate on these topics if its general powers of delegated legislation were extended in these areas to include power to amend Acts of Parliament (by so-called 'Henry VIII clauses'); but this would need safeguards and might require confirmation by Westminster.

Legislative Devolution

Legislative power could be devolved in all subjects currently the responsibility of the Welsh Office. Westminster would need to retain a degree of legislative responsibility in three circumstances: to protect the interests of the rest of the UK; to enforce international obligations; and to protect the integrity of the common legal system. Westminster would still be able to legislate even in devolved subject areas, because of the supremacy of parliament; but the history of the Northern Ireland Parliament at Stormont suggests such intervention would be rare.

There could be **phased devolution** with the transfer of legislative power in stages, on the model of the Northern Ireland Constitution Act 1973. Legislative power might initially be conferred in such fields as local government, housing, Welsh language, arts and culture; and gradually be extended to education, health, social services, etc.

The legislation could:
- define the powers reserved to Westminster (as in the Government of Ireland Act 1920); or
- define the legislative powers devolved to the Assembly (as in the Scotland Act 1978).
It is easier to define the powers reserved; but this would not be possible with phased devolution, which would have to define the legislative power transferred at each stage.

Structure of the Assembly

The Wales Act 1978 conferred executive power on the Assembly and its committees following the **local government model**. The Assembly was required to establish multi-party committees, with the leaders of the committees forming an overall Executive Committee. The local government model involves all members in decision making; but it has been criticised for its cumbersome committee structure, slow decision taking, diffusion of responsibility, and relegation of real policy making to the party caucus.

A more effective alternative could be the **cabinet model,** with an executive separate from the Assembly. This produces quicker decisions and sharper accountability, but gives less of a role for backbenchers.

The Assembly and Central Government

The Secretary of State for Wales will have a vital role in implementing the devolution legislation and setting up the Assembly and Welsh Executive. He or she will also help to establish smooth working relations between the new Welsh government and Whitehall. Thereafter the office is largely redundant: the Welsh administration will deal direct with Whitehall departments. Any residual liaison function could transfer to a Minister with overall responsibility for relations with the nations and regions of the UK.

The question of Welsh representation at Westminster is likely to arise just as sharply as it did in the 1970s. It cannot be ignored, particularly since Wales is already over-represented (at 40 seats after the next election, when its share proportionate to population would be 33). It would be wrong to exclude Welsh MPs altogether; and impracticable to allow them to vote only on non-devolved matters. One response may be to offer a review of Scottish and Welsh representation once the devolved Assemblies are established; another would be to wait until after any referendum is held on the electoral system for the House of Commons.

The new Welsh administration should initially be part of the home civil service, but could later establish a separate Welsh civil service.

Quangos

The creation of a Welsh Assembly will provide the opportunity to review the whole framework and accountability of quangos. They have caused public concern in Wales because of their inadequate accountability; the nature of appointments to their boards; and lapses in their internal management. But it is only a few high profile executive bodies which have given rise to that concern. In many areas there are sound reasons for retaining quangos with a degree of operational independence. The majority are specialist bodies operating in technical fields where the government needs independent expertise and advice.

The Assembly and Local Government

Constructive relations between the Assembly and local government could be greatly helped by:
- a new agreement about the system of local government finance.
- a concordat respecting the role of each tier, and consultative and other procedures.
- co-option of local authority members onto Assembly committees.
- dual membership permitting councillors to stand for the Assembly.

Europe

The Welsh Assembly and Executive will want to maximise Welsh influence in Brussels. This will continue to be done largely through UK Ministers and departments, because the UK is the member state. The Welsh Executive will need to negotiate a co-operation agreement with the UK government providing for:
- a continuing flow of information.
- participation in preparatory meetings.
- the right to send observers to working group and Council meetings on devolved matters.

The Welsh Assembly will need to establish procedures for monitoring and scrutiny of developments in Europe. It should welcome the Welsh MEPs and co-opt them onto its European Affairs Committee.

Electoral System

All parties envisage an Assembly of 80-100 members. Labour has proposed elections by 'first past the post', and the Liberal Democrats and Plaid Cymru by proportional representation. 'First past the post' is more concerned with producing strong government, and proportional representation with producing a representative Assembly. A 'first past the post' system may not be necessary where one party is already dominant. Proportional representation has been proposed to offer a sense of involvement to the minority parties and to quell fears that the Assembly will be dominated by Labour and the interests of South Wales.

The Liberal Democrats have proposed using the single transferable vote, already used for certain elections in Northern Ireland; and Plaid Cymru the additional member system, which is the system proposed for the Scottish Parliament. Different features of the two systems are:
STV
- emphasises fairness to voters not to parties.
- enables voters to discriminate between candidates of the same party.
- gives a better chance to independents.
- requires multi-member constituencies.
AMS
- retains single member constituencies.
- follows the analogy with Scotland.
- gives power to the political parties in drawing up the party lists.

The Assembly is unlikely to sit more than 100 days a year, so that membership of the Welsh Assembly may not be a full-time occupation. There should be no restriction on MPs and local government councillors standing for election. Dual membership can be left to find its own level determined by the workload and the views of constituents.

Finance

Additional staff will be required for the Assembly itself; to service the Executive Members; to manage the split with the Secretary of State, and greater separation from Whitehall; to respond to additional demands from the Assembly; and the greater expectations of the public. It is difficult to quantify how many additional staff would be required; in the 1970s the estimate was 1,150. Every 100 additional staff of the Welsh administration will cost around £3m. The annual running costs of the Assembly itself have been estimated at around £15m.

In the long term devolution may require a change to the whole system of determining public expenditure in Wales. The current system whereby the Treasury determines the Welsh block (the 'Barnett formula') may not survive the greater scrutiny involved in an external transfer mechanism between governments. It may need to be replaced with a regular needs assessment exercise conducted by an independent Commission whose recommendations for the territorial shares would be debated annually in Parliament.

If the Welsh Assembly is to have responsibility for making real choices about the level and nature of public spending in Wales it will need power to raise some of its own revenue. The yield may not be significant, and it may create the gearing problems evident with local government; but without some revenue raising power the Welsh Assembly will have no fiscal accountability to the Welsh people. This might be a power which needs to be conferred later, once the Assembly has become established.

Resolution of Disputes

Any division of powers between a Welsh Assembly and the Westminster Parliament will ultimately depend upon legal interpretation in the courts. The devolution legislation must provide for the possibility of challenge to the validity of legislation passed by the Welsh Assembly. Upon introduction of a bill the Speaker or Clerk to the Welsh Assembly should certify that the bill was within the Assembly's competence. Upon enactment there should be the possibility of a fast-track reference to the courts. This could be to the Judicial Committee of the Privy Council (as proposed in 1978) or to the Appellate Committee of the House of Lords. To prevent uncertainty at the apex of the legal system it seems preferable for the final court of appeal on devolution issues to be the House of Lords.

Entrenchment

It is impossible within the Westminster tradition of sovereignty to find satisfactory ways of formally entrenching the powers or the existence of the Welsh Assembly. More effective than legal entrenchment might be political entrenchment by a referendum. If a referendum is offered, it might be better to hold it in advance of the legislation (as proposed for Northern Ireland) rather than afterwards (as happened in 1978). It could help decide the question of principle whether Wales wants an Assembly. It would need to be based upon a clear White Paper; and enabling legislation would be required to authorise holding the referendum.

A second form of political entrenchment would be to strengthen Welsh representation at Westminster, not in the House of Commons but in a reformed House of Lords. This could not apply to Wales alone. A House of Lords remodelled on the lines of second chambers such as the German Bundesrat could play a significant part in protecting the interest of the nations and regions and in helping to maintain the Union.

The Timetable for Implementation

Scotland dominated the devolution debates in the 1970s. In the 1990s Wales risks being overshadowed by Scotland again. The risk is that much greater if both devolution bills are introduced in the same session. If the government wished to allow time for a separate debate in Wales the Welsh legislation could be brought forward later.

The timetable for introducing devolution legislation to Wales will depend on:
● the political priority attached to it.
● the links with Scotland.
● the way the legislation is framed.
● whether there is a referendum held in advance.

A referendum would require separate legislation; if this passed swiftly the overall timetable might be delayed by six months or so. In the 1970s it took over two years to prepare the first Scotland and Wales Bill. The timetable for a new government would depend upon how quickly Cabinet colleagues and Whitehall departments could agree the contents of a new Wales Bill.

Chapter 1

Introduction

> "Cardiff
> swirls about the numb
> and calm cube of its castle cliff:
> rune of departed power for some,
> to others towers a hieroglyph
> of sovereign power to come
> if if."
>
> Raymond Garlick, 'A Sense of Time'.

The Constitution Unit and Devolution

1   This report on a Welsh Assembly is one of three reports by the Constitution Unit on devolution, published at the same time as related reports on a Scottish Parliament and on Regional Government in England. This report does not seek to draw up a blueprint for a Welsh Assembly. The Constitution Unit is conducting a technical inquiry into the implementation of constitutional reform, aiming to identify the practical difficulties facing a reforming Government in introducing a Welsh Assembly, and possible solutions to those difficulties. Our starting point is the policies of the political parties, which are set out at the end of this chapter.

2   The report is divided into four parts:
   • the first part gives the political background, describing the history of previous proposals, the lessons to be learnt from the failed attempt at devolution in the 1970s, and concludes with a possible set of objectives for a Welsh Assembly in the 1990s.
   • the second part sets out the considerations and the options which will determine the role and functions of the Assembly, its composition and powers.
   • the third part describes the relations between the Assembly and other levels of government: central government, quangos, local government and the European Union.
   • the fourth part discusses finance, dispute resolution, legislation and the necessary transitional arrangements.

The Political Background

Gladstone and Liberal Home Rule

3   Proposals for a Welsh Parliament or Assembly go back roughly one hundred years. England and Wales have been a single political unit for some five hundred years: the gradual integration which took place during the fourteenth and fifteenth centuries was completed by the Tudor Acts of Union of 1536 and 1543. After that time, Wales was administered as part of England. "The distinction between England and Wales" Gladstone claimed, "...is totally unknown to our constitution"[1].

4   It was in Gladstone's time that a political distinction began to emerge. The extension of the franchise in 1867 and 1884 had brought politics to the Welsh for the first time. The Liberals' support for home rule for Ireland led to Liberal interest in home rule for Scotland and Wales as well. Tom Ellis, the founder of Cymru Fydd (Wales of the Future), declared in his election address at Merioneth in 1886: "I solicit your suffrages as a Welsh nationalist"[2]; and Lloyd George was to describe himself as a radical and Welsh nationalist.

5   This nationalism did not entail separatism, for Cymru Fydd called for home rule within the United Kingdom. By the early 1890s, backed by Lloyd George and Alfred Thomas, there were proposals to put a top tier on the new system of County Councils in order to consider matters of common interest to Wales, to create a devolved Executive for Wales and to appoint a Secretary of State. In 1891 the Liberal Party committed itself to Welsh disestablishment, Ellis became a junior Whip and Lloyd George urged home rule for Wales.

6   It was not to be, for three connected reasons. The Welsh Liberals were divided on the question of home rule; the divisions grew with the industrialisation of South Wales; and industrialisation led to the collapse of the Liberal Party. The Liberals were chiefly interested in disestablishment of the Welsh church and creating educational institutions for Wales rather than a Welsh Parliament. As early as 1898, D.A.Thomas turned the South Wales Liberals against home rule. With their growing connections with London and the Midlands, the industrial English speaking valleys of the South placed greater emphasis on labour and industrial questions than the rural and Welsh speaking North. After the First World War, and then with the slump of the 1930s, the valleys and the Welsh heartland turned to Labour, and Labour displaced the Liberals as the dominant political party in Wales.

7   The Welsh nationalist movement was left to the rural areas and linked with the cultural symbols of land, religion and language. In 1925 Plaid Cymru was created, but under the leadership of Saunders Lewis it became a movement to preserve the Welsh language, a cultural conservationist society rather than a political party. This emphasis on the language confined Plaid's appeal to Welsh speaking Wales and proved deeply divisive; promotion of the language did nothing to help Plaid's aim of self-government for Wales.

Labour's First Thoughts: an All-Wales Council

8   Plaid Cymru's political breakthrough came in the 1960s, when Gwynfor Evans captured Carmarthen from Labour in the general election of 1966. His triumph coincided with the second occasion when the governing party considered the possibility of an elected Assembly. The steady growth of central government had led most Ministries in Whitehall to establish Welsh divisions or departments; and after the Second World War the Government had established an advisory council for Wales, and then in 1951 a Minister for Welsh Affairs. Initially this was the Home Secretary; in 1957 a separate Minister of State was appointed as the first full-time Minister for Wales. In 1964 the new Labour Government upgraded this post to Secretary of State with a seat in the Cabinet, and established the Welsh Office as a separate department.

9   The following year the Welsh Labour Party committed itself to an Assembly, for two reasons with a modern ring: to make ad hoc nominated bodies (not yet called quangos) more accountable, and to provide a second tier all-Wales Council as part of a wider re-organisation of local government. An inter-departmental working party set up by the Welsh Office made a similar proposal. The Council would have been a super-local authority, not assuming any of the powers of central government. The first two Secretaries of State for Wales, James Griffiths and Cledwyn Hughes, were both sympathetic to an elected Welsh Council; but the proposal was defeated in Cabinet by William Ross (Secretary of State for Scotland) and James Callaghan. Ross feared it would become impossible to resist the demand for a Scottish Parliament if Wales had its own Assembly; Callaghan feared it would provide a forum for Plaid Cymru, and was reflecting the hostility to local government re-organisation from the constituency Labour parties in Cardiff[3].

10   Labour had inherited the ambivalent attitude of the Liberals to Welsh national claims, albeit for different reasons. With its strength in Scotland and in Wales, one of Labour's roles was to articulate the old radical grievances against the centre. But whereas the Liberals had emphasised the dispersal of power, the Labour Party, through its programmes of nationalisation and economic planning, was essentially an agent of centralisation. In office in 1945 and again in

1964 Labour's main concerns lay in economic planning and social reform. It believed in stronger government in London, to deliver universal benefits throughout the UK. This centralist philosophy came into conflict with Labour's other role as the party of peripheral protest, and the voice of the Celtic fringe.

Labour's Next Try: the Wales Act 1978

11   This conflict became acute under the Labour Government of 1974-79 when the third and closest attempt was made to establish an Assembly for Wales. The drive came from Scotland, where the Scottish National Party had made inroads into the Labour vote far more threatening than Plaid Cymru in Wales. Labour could not dismiss the nationalist claims out of hand, and in 1968 announced a Royal Commission on the Constitution, chaired first by Lord Crowther and then after his death by Lord Kilbrandon. The Royal Commission reported in late 1973, six months before Labour returned to power in February 1974. The members of the Commission were seriously divided, being unanimous only in rejecting separatism, federalism and the status quo. Something was rotten in the state of the United Kingdom, and some kind of devolutionist response was required, but the Commissioners could not agree what: their report offered six alternative schemes of devolution.

12   The Labour Government elected in February 1974 could not afford to hedge its bets or to play for time. The Scottish nationalists had gained six seats and Plaid Cymru two, and Harold Wilson took office as head of a minority Government which needed support from the nationalists and the Liberals. It rushed out a Green Paper in June and a White Paper in September 1974[4], three weeks before the second general election in that year. The Government announced that there would be directly elected Assemblies for Scotland and Wales, with the Scottish Assembly having legislative powers while the Welsh Assembly would have executive powers only. The Assemblies would be financed mainly through block grant allocated by the UK Treasury. Contrary to the Royal Commission's recommendations, there was to be no reduction in the number of Scottish or Welsh MPs, and the Secretaries of State for Scotland and Wales would continue to have places in the Cabinet.

13   These decisions in principle formed the basis of the Labour Government's devolution policy. Although the policy was refined and amended in four subsequent White Papers, the broad outline remained unchanged. It was a minimalist devolution policy, with no legislative powers for the Welsh Assembly; no revenue raising powers; with Whitehall retaining responsibility for economic and industrial matters, energy and agriculture; and significant override powers for the Secretary of State, whose functions were likened by its critics to those of a Governor General.

14   There is not space to record the many reverses and changes of tack forced upon the Government by a series of parliamentary defeats. The Government was forced to concede a referendum, which had been stoutly resisted; the first Scotland and Wales Bill had to be withdrawn when the Government's guillotine motion was defeated. It was only thanks to the Lib/Lab pact that the devolution legislation was revived, with separate Bills for Scotland and Wales; and in the last year of the Labour Government the Scotland Act and the Wales Act 1978 both finally reached the statute book.

15   Thanks to a backbench amendment the Acts could only come into force if approved on a referendum by 40% of those eligible to vote in Scotland and Wales. Expectations of a general

election in the autumn of 1978 delayed the referendum until the spring. When it was eventually held on 1 March 1979, St David's Day, the people of Wales decisively rejected the Assembly proposed in the Wales Act by four to one.

16 Such a heavy defeat had not been forecast by the opinion polls, which had shown Welsh opinion fairly evenly divided all through the devolution debates of the 1970s. A number of factors contributed to the result[5]. After the winter of discontent, the Government's standing was very low. The Welsh Labour Party was deeply divided, with 6 Labour MPs (including Leo Abse and Neil Kinnock) campaigning strongly against. Instead of forming a strong cross-party campaign, the 'Yes' campaigners divided into different factions. The recent local government re-organisation had not settled down, the new counties came out against, and a Welsh Assembly seemed one tier of government too many. And finally, a feature that had dogged Welsh politics since Gladstone's day, the people of the North feared domination by the South; and the people of the South feared the Assembly would be taken over by Plaid Cymru and the Welsh language speakers of the West and North.

Political Developments since 1979

17 Now, in the mid-1990s, polling evidence shows a resurgence of support for a Welsh Assembly. What has happened? The most obvious feature is 17 years of Conservative Government. Wales has never voted Conservative, giving its allegiance first to the Liberals and for most of this century to the Labour Party. The sense of English domination has been strong, with a series of English Secretaries of State appointed to rule in Wales. Employment in coal and steel, the mainstay of South Wales has substantially declined; and the Welsh economy has undergone a brutal transformation.

18 Gone are the days of heavy industry, and in its place has come technology and light industry with high levels of foreign investment. By 1991, 25,000 people in Wales worked in electronics compared to 20,000 in mining and steel, while 70,000 worked in financial services. Over 400 foreign-owned manufacturing companies in Wales employed around 70,000 people, almost 30% of the Welsh manufacturing workforce. The growth in professional and financial services has also helped generally to boost local confidence: the Welsh business community is more self-sufficient, and need no longer feel so dependent on London for legal or financial advice.

19 Sweeping changes have been introduced to the system of government, with the introduction and abolition of the poll tax, privatisation of the public utilities, and removal of important functions of central and local government to boards and quangos whose members are not elected but appointed by the Secretary of State. The Welsh Language Act 1993 has taken some of the heat out of the Welsh language issue. Wales has become an enthusiastic participant in the European Union, developing strong partnerships with elected regional governments in other member States. Finally, and most recently, there has been a further re-organisation of local government, with the introduction of unitary authorities throughout Wales; so that for the first time it is possible to envisage the second tier being provided by an elected regional government in the form of a Welsh Assembly.

The Position of the Political Parties

20   All that remains is to summarise the current position of the major political parties on the question of a Welsh Assembly; and to summarise what is known about public opinion.

Conservative Party

21   The Conservatives remain stoutly opposed. In their most recent briefing document (*Conservative Research Department Brief on Constitutional Matters*, February 1996) they state:
> "The Conservative and Unionist Party is the only Party which is firmly committed to securing political and economic progress in Wales within the existing constitutional arrangements. Home rule, in any form, would sooner or later lead to constitutional conflict or deadlock, undermining the Union with England, Scotland, and Northern Ireland that serves Welsh interests so well... In Wales, as in the rest of the United Kingdom, the Conservative Party has consistently advocated a very different form of devolution. Over the last sixteen years, this Government has moved power and responsibility for local services closer to the people who use them, ensuring that decisions are taken by individuals - and local bodies such as schools, hospitals and housing estates - rather than by bureaucrats in the Town Hall".

22   In his introduction to a 1994 version, John Redwood added:
> "An Assembly in Cardiff would be a disaster. It would centralise power when it should be dispersed. It would charge you for the privilege of being Welsh. It would take powers on planning, on roads, on education away from local people and their Councils. Surely five layers of government is more than enough without any more? The world's business would go somewhere else to avoid the extra Welsh laws and taxes".[6]

23   His successor, William Hague, has since announced plans for strengthening the accountability of Welsh Ministers to Parliament by breathing life into the Welsh Grand Committee (which consists of all the Welsh MPs and five English MPs). In future other Cabinet Ministers are to appear before the Grand Committee to answer questions on Welsh matters; and there are to be at least four meetings a year, with some held outside Cardiff. If a recent Procedure Committee report is accepted, proceedings of the Grand Committee may also be in Welsh when it is meeting in Wales.

Labour Party

24   After its defeat at the 1992 general election, the Wales Labour Party established a policy commission to re-examine and update the Party's policy on a Welsh Assembly. The commission issued a consultation paper and organised six public consultation meetings to ascertain what type of Assembly would command the broadest range of support in Wales. In May 1995, the Wales Labour Party published the conclusions of this exercise in its policy document *Shaping the Vision: A Report on the Powers and Structure of the Welsh Assembly,* and in May 1996 it published a second report *Preparing for a New Wales* outlining how the Assembly would work in practice.

25 Labour is pledged to legislate to establish an Assembly within a year of coming into office.[7] Apart from reflecting the wider powers now enjoyed by the Welsh Office, its proposals are very similar to the 1970s model:
- the Assembly would take responsibility for the existing budget of the Welsh Office and its functions, with responsibilities in the fields of agriculture, industry and economic development, employment and training, education, the Welsh language, arts and recreation, transport, local government and housing, environmental services and health.
- the Assembly would have power to make secondary legislation within the terms of primary legislation passed by Westminster.
- the Secretary of State for Wales should have a statutory duty to consult with the Assembly on Westminster's legislative programme for the coming year.
- the Assembly should review and restructure all quangos in Wales, with major reform of all the big executive quangos, and possible creation of a single economic development agency whose board would be appointed by the Assembly.
- funding by central government grant based on a guaranteed equalisation formula.
- elections to be by 'first past the post' with fixed terms of four years.
- the Assembly to operate on the local government model, with subject committees reflecting overall party balance responsible for developing policy and overseeing the work of departments.
- the Assembly to establish regional committees to liaise with local authorities, and to be under a duty to maintain a vibrant and independent system of local government.
- an executive committee to be formed by the committee leaders, and chaired by the leader of the majority party in the Assembly.
- no reduction in the number of Welsh MPs at Westminster, with MPs participating in all non-devolved matters.
- a strong and continuing role for the Secretary of State, who would represent Wales in Cabinet, negotiate the budget of the Welsh Assembly, and attend meetings of the European Council of Ministers.
- no need for a referendum, because the electorate would have expressed their clear choice at the general election.

Liberal Democrats

26 The Welsh Liberal Democrats' most recent policy statement (*A Senedd for Wales: Beyond a Talking Shop*) was issued in April 1996 and approved at their spring conference in May. It begins by recording the Liberals' long history of support for decentralisation and home rule, and commits the Liberal Democrats to introduce legislation for a Welsh Senedd in the first year of a new Government. Specifically:
- the Senedd would be part of a UK federal structure which could eventually include the English regions.
- it would have approximately 100 members elected by single transferable vote.
- it would have primary legislative powers in all fields covered by the Welsh Office, plus overseas trade and law and order.
- the Senedd would have power to raise or lower the rate of income tax by up to 3%.
- the powers and functions of local government would be entrenched against encroachment by the Senedd.
- the post of Welsh Secretary would become obsolete as soon as the Senedd was operational.

- the number of Welsh MPs at Westminster would be reduced to take account of their reduced role in the light of the establishment of the Senedd.
- a constitutional court would be set up to deal with disputes between the Senedd and the Westminster Parliament, and a Welsh supreme court to head the judicial system in Wales.
- the Senedd would maintain its own relations with other European States, and have direct representation in the European Council of Ministers.

Plaid Cymru

27   Plaid Cymru's policy is one of evolution towards self-government for Wales within the European Union rather than outright independence. In 1987 it adopted as an interim objective the creation of a Welsh Senedd, and its latest policy document (*A Democratic Wales in a United Europe*, September 1995) elaborated its proposals as follows:
- a two-chamber Welsh Parliament, with a 100 member House of Representatives and a 44 member Congress.
- the House of Representatives to be elected by proportional representation, the Congress to consist of two representatives from each of the 22 local authorities.
- the Parliament to legislate in all areas except those reserved for Westminster: defence and international affairs, monetary policy and banking, control of currency and exchange rates, international trade, patents and social security.
- Welsh representation in the House of Commons to remain unchanged, but Welsh MPs could only vote on the reserved matters listed above, or on votes of confidence, or on supply votes.
- equal representation of men and women in both House of Representatives and Congress.
- Welsh and English languages to have legal and effective equal status.
- the Parliament of Wales to have the sole right to raise taxes, with a contribution to the UK Government to finance the reserved matters.
- an integrated public service with transferability between the civil service, local government and those employed by quangos.
- a separate court structure for Wales.
- a right of direct representation to the EU and observer status in all meetings of the EU Council of Ministers.
- after five years the Welsh Parliament would have powers to call down the reserved functions so that Wales would become a self-governing state within the European Union. That decision would be for the people of Wales to decide through the ballot box.

The Parliament for Wales Campaign (Ymgyrch Senedd Cymru)

28   The Parliament for Wales Campaign (Ymgyrch Senedd Cymru) articulated its policy for a Welsh Parliament with effective legislative and financial powers in 1994 in the Llandrindod Wells *Democracy Declaration*. By the device of drafting a *Government of Wales Bill* (1996) it has developed its proposals in more detailed form than the political parties. Its principal proposals are:
- a single chamber Senedd of 100 members elected for 4 years.
- elections to be by single transferable vote based on 20 constituencies, each returning 5 members.
- an Executive Council (Y Gyngor Gweithredol) of 9-11 drawn from, and accountable to, the Senedd.

- the Senedd to have legislative powers for the good government of Wales, except for matters expressly reserved for Westminster: the Crown, defence and foreign affairs, taxation, currency and bank rate, social security, immigration, companies, insurance and pensions, etc.
- the Senedd to have power to vary personal income tax and VAT by up to 3%, but only from its second term.
- differences over jurisdiction to be resolved between the Secretary of State and the Executive Council, failing which the matter to be referred to the Judicial Committee of the Privy Council.
- the Senedd not to legislate incompatibly with EU law; the Secretary of State to have power to intervene to resolve differences, or failing agreement to refer the matter to the European Court of Justice.
- a member of the Welsh Executive to have a right to accompany UK representatives to EU meetings where Welsh interests are affected and the opportunity to represent the UK where Welsh interests are principally in issue.
- departmental committees to be set up by the Senedd, with cross-party membership, to be consulted by the relevant Minister on general policy and legislation, and to monitor the activities of the department concerned.
- funding of public expenditure to be by a block grant, less income tax and VAT raised in Wales; the block grant to be negotiated by a Joint Exchequer Board comprising representatives of the Welsh Executive and the Treasury.
- the quangos in receipt of Government funds to be subject to scrutiny by the Senedd Public Accounts Committee; appointments to all quangos to be made by the Senedd on the advice of the Executive Council after considering the views of the Commissioner for Public Appointments for Wales.
- establishment of a Welsh public service with provision for free movement between it and the UK Civil Service and local authorities.
- transfer of Home Office functions relating to prisons, probation and the fire service to the Executive Council.
- Welsh MPs in the UK Parliament to remain at 40, but not to have a vote on essentially English or Scottish matters, unless involving an issue of confidence.
- the Senedd to establish a commission to review local government organisation in Wales.

Public Opinion in Wales

29 This last section briefly reports what is known about public opinion in Wales towards a Welsh Assembly, by summarising the two most recent opinion surveys. The feeling at Westminster is that Wales is still ambivalent about the Assembly. This is partially borne out by the survey data. In March 1996, HTV commissioned NOP to ask about the level of support for an Assembly and what powers it should have. From a sample of 1450 respondents, 45% were in favour of the establishment of an elected Assembly, 31% against and 24% did not know. Support was stronger amongst the younger age groups and the lower socio-economic groups. When those not in favour or undecided were asked about the impact of a Scottish Parliament, a further 12% came out in favour of an Assembly for Wales.

30 The 1,000 or so respondents who were originally in favour or undecided were then asked four further questions about the elected Assembly:

Table 1 What Kind of Assembly do the Welsh People Want?

Question	Yes	No	Don't know
Limited law making powers	52%	21%	27%
Limited tax raising powers	50%	22%	27%
Elect by proportional representation	57%	9%	34%
Endorse by referendum	70%	5%	24%

Source: NOP Social and Political, March 1996

A referendum is normally associated with those opposed to an Assembly: here it is being supported by those in favour (or undecided). Another point of note is that the responses of Labour supporters to these four questions matched those of the sample as a whole.

31 The other recent survey comes from Beaufort Research, who conduct regular opinion surveys using about 1,000 interviewees in Wales. The figures from the last three surveys on views for and against an Assembly are as follows:

Table 2 Level of Support for a Welsh Assembly

Date	For	Against	Don't know
November 1994	51%	19%	30%
June 1995	41%	21%	37%
November 1995	42%	20%	38%

Source: Beaufort Research, January 1996

The number of don't knows is quite high. On a regional breakdown there is not a huge amount of variation across Wales. Those in favour outnumber those against in all parts of Wales, with the strongest support in mid and west Wales and the lowest support in South Glamorgan and Gwent.

32 For the November 1995 survey the Institute of Welsh Affairs commissioned Beaufort Research to ask some more detailed questions, putting to respondents half a dozen arguments for and against a Welsh Assembly. The survey concluded that respondents considered the most important objective for an Assembly to be:
● to bring more investment and jobs to Wales (37%).
● to provide Wales with a stronger and more independent political voice (19%).
● to make the Welsh Office and quangos more directly accountable (12%).
Of the arguments against a Welsh Assembly, the most important concerns were:
● the increased cost of government in Wales (21%).
● the possible break up of the UK (17%).
● dominance by Welsh language interests (15%).

33   Respondents were also asked about a referendum, with a similar result to the NOP poll. 9% thought the vote at a general election provided sufficient authority for the creation of a Welsh Assembly, and 71% thought the people of Wales should be consulted in a referendum first.

Conclusion

34   This chapter has set the scene by describing the history of previous proposals for a Welsh Assembly and the positions of the main political parties. Three times in the last 100 years the possibility of a Welsh Assembly has been put on the political agenda: first by Lloyd George in the 1890s, next by the Labour Government in its private deliberations in the 1960s, and finally when an Assembly was legislated for by the last Labour Government in the 1970s. The legislation was repealed after it was decisively rejected on a referendum in 1979.

35   Labour, the Liberal Democrats and Plaid Cymru all support the creation of a Welsh Assembly. Labour's proposed Assembly would have executive powers and be elected by 'first past the post.' The Liberal Democrats and Plaid Cymru both propose a Senedd with law making powers to be elected by proportional representation. The Conservatives remain opposed to the creation of a Welsh Assembly.

36   Public opinion surveys in Wales suggest some 45% are in favour of an Assembly with 30% against and 25% don't knows. Of the 70% in favour and undecided, 50% want an Assembly with limited legislative and revenue raising power, 60% want proportional representation, and 70% want a referendum on the issue.

Chapter 2

Lessons from the 1970s

Introduction

37   This chapter begins by describing the political difficulties facing the Labour Government in the 1970s and the reasons for the peculiar nature of the devolution debate in Wales. It identifies the main issues in the 1979 referendum campaign which led to the proposals in the Wales Act 1978 being decisively rejected. The second part of the chapter contains a critique of the 1978 Act as a scheme of executive devolution. It identifies a number of serious weaknesses in the scheme and concludes that it might have proved difficult to operate if it had ever been brought into force.

The Political Background

38   The events surrounding the devolution debate in the 1970s might seem to have little relevance to the circumstances of the 1990s. The Labour Government 1974-79 was particularly weak and susceptible to events. Its slim and disappearing majority rendered it vulnerable to its own backbenchers and, eventually, enabled it to govern only thanks to the Lib/Lab pact. It was against this backdrop that the Government's devolution policy was developed by a Cabinet which was deeply divided on the issue, and not fully in control of Parliament or its own backbenchers. The Government could not afford to alienate the nationalists or the Liberals, and rushed out first a Green Paper and then a White Paper on devolution before the October 1974 election. The Scottish Parliament would have legislative powers while the Welsh Assembly was to have executive power only.

39   Despite the unusual political background, there are a number of lessons which can be learnt from the devolution debate of the 1970s:
   • the dominance of Scotland.
   • the intra-party divisions.
   • the unreality of the parliamentary debates.
   • the poor quality of the public debate.
   • the confused issues in the referendum campaign.

The Dominance of Scotland

40   Although the emergence of nationalism on the political agenda was initially brought about by Plaid Cymru's 1960s success in Welsh by-elections, it was the threat posed by the SNP in the 1970s which obliged Labour to confront the issue. As a result of the relative strength of the SNP and the relative weakness of Plaid Cymru in the two general elections in 1974, the devolution debate was dominated by Scotland: by the perceived threat posed by the SNP to the integrity of the UK; and by the proposal to devolve extensive political powers to an elected Scottish Parliament.

41   The Scottish dominance extended to the parliamentary arena. The initial devolution Bill encompassed both Scotland and Wales and was introduced as a very complex piece of legislation to Parliament in November 1976. This combined Bill proved to be politically dangerous for the Government. It enabled those Scottish and Welsh backbenchers who opposed devolution, for reasons largely unique to Scotland or to Wales, to band together to such good effect that the Government was forced to abandon the Bill when it failed to carry a guillotine motion in February 1977 (with 45 Labour MPs abstaining or voting against the Government).

42   Two separate Bills were then prepared, one for Scotland and one for Wales. Both were introduced in November 1977, progressed in tandem through the Commons, proceeded to the House of Lords in May 1978 and subsequently received the Royal Assent in July 1978. Both in the passage of the original Scotland and Wales Bill and the subsequent separate Bills, the debate on Scottish clauses preceded that on Welsh clauses. Thus the Government's policy on devolution, as transmitted by the media and as perceived by the general public, was largely that concerned with Scotland. The issues of the Welsh devolution debate were given very little coverage outside Wales (despite the differences, the two debates appeared repetitive so that the second was deemed not newsworthy). Furthermore, even within Wales, the dominance of the London press with total morning daily sales of 700,000 compared with less than 150,000 for the Welsh morning dailies meant that the Welsh debate failed to reach most Welsh electors.[8] Nor was this deficiency overcome by the broadcasting media. While both BBC Wales and HTV Wales scheduled a wide range of devolution and referendum programmes, the national news programmes reflected the dominance of Scottish devolution in the referendum debate. The different provisions for Welsh devolution, including its limited character compared to Scotland were not fully explained or appreciated.

The Unreality of the Parliamentary Debates

43   The parliamentary debates on the Wales Bill suffered from another weakness. They had an unreal quality. Every MP knew that the Labour Government's concession of a referendum meant that the final decision would rest with the Welsh electorate. Consequently, debates did not move beyond general discussions about the principles of devolution, rhetoric tended to replace argument and speeches were made to set down markers for the forthcoming referendum. These included amendments designed to show that the Bill :
- was the first step on the road to the secession of Wales from the United Kingdom.
- would increase bureaucracy and corruption.
- would lead to the domination of a Welsh speaking elite.

44   There was another element to the parliamentary passage of the Bill which had implications for the broader political debate. Constitutional reform, then as now, does not sit easily with the party political divide. During the passage of the Wales Bill very strange alliances were struck. Government backbenchers and Opposition backbenchers equally hostile to devolution supported each others' amendments and established informal channels to liaise on tactics and strategy. These contacts led to charges being raised in the referendum that some MPs were traitors to Wales, or to the party or both. Feelings ran particularly high in the Welsh Labour Party, with bitter personal attacks on the so-called 'gang of six' Labour backbenchers who were opposed to devolution.

45   This meant that the Wales Act which should have been the central focus of the political debate became obscured. The general public and many of the political activists were largely ignorant of the details of the Act and of the specific and limited powers which the proposed Welsh Assembly would exercise.

The Issues in the Referendum Campaign

46   During the course of the referendum campaign three major issues emerged which dominated the debate and arguably determined its outcome:

- the debate on costs. There were a number of strands to the debate. First, it was feared that Wales would lose out in the allocation of funding and that a Westminster Parliament would be less generous if devolution took place. Second, it was suggested that the Assembly's role in negotiating the level of the rate support grant would undermine the influence of local government, and any increase would not necessarily be passed on to the local authorities. Third, the cost of running the Assembly (estimated by the 'No' campaigners at £20m a year) was presented as money taken from the people to pay bureaucrats. By the end of the campaign the majority of the electorate appeared to conclude that a Welsh Assembly was an unnecessary extravagance.

- the linguistic divide emerged as a divisive factor and tended to reinforce the North/South divide in Welsh politics. Thus on the one hand the Assembly was presented as "tailor made for the Labour Party caucus in South Wales" (*Western Mail*, 23 March 1979) while on the other hand it was suspected that the Assembly would be dominated by a Welsh speaking, and largely North Wales, linguistic elite. In one particularly evocative speech, Leo Abse warned that "the English speaking majority [in Wales] would be condemned to be strangers in their own land". [9]

- local government interests also influenced the campaign. Initially the unpopularity of the Conservative local government reforms in Wales led many commentators to anticipate that these issues would benefit the pro-devolutionists. However the reverse happened. The new local authorities rapidly acquired interests which they feared might be threatened by an elected Assembly. Similarly, local authority unions accepted that further changes in Welsh administration might adversely affect their members. By the end of the campaign the local government establishment in Wales was almost universally hostile to the implementation of the Wales Act. The 'No' campaigners had successfully argued that the Act far from devolving power down would, in effect, centralise power in Cardiff and away from the local communities in Wales.

47   The final, and possibly most significant, determining issue was the slippery-slope argument; that the Assembly would inevitably come into conflict with Westminster, claim the authority of Welsh nationhood and move towards an increasingly separatist position. [10] This was a fear expressed not just by the Conservatives, for there were sincere unionists in both parties: the Conservatives whose unionism was steeped in the constitutional doctrine of the sovereignty of Parliament; and Labour MPs for whom maintenance of a strong central government was essential to deliver Labour's policies of economic planning and social welfare.

48   Although the precise form of devolution provided for in the Wales Act was not a salient feature in the campaign, there is some evidence that it may have been a factor in its rejection in the referendum. Two polls commissioned by BBC Wales and published during the referendum campaign revealed that the limited form of executive devolution envisaged in the Wales Act was the least liked of all the devolution options. Both legislative devolution and complete self-government commanded greater support than executive devolution.

49   There is also further evidence that the provisions of the Wales Act failed to attract the enthusiastic support of Government Ministers. Lord Crowther-Hunt considered the Act to be so inadequate that he concluded "it must amount to sabotage by the drafters in London" *(Western Mail,* 28 February 1979). That was a serious criticism coming from the adviser (and later a Minister) who had been the main architect of the Government's devolution policy in 1974-76. It was also grossly unfair because, as we shall see in the next section, the Wales Act was the logical conclusion of a scheme of executive devolution: a scheme for which Lord Crowther-Hunt, as the lead author of the 1974 White Paper, must bear his share of responsibility.

A Critique of the Wales Act 1978

50   The Wales Act would have established a scheme of executive devolution only. Unlike its Scottish counterpart, the elected Assembly was given no powers to enact primary legislation. The Act transferred to the Assembly a series of statutory functions, precisely enumerated in the Act, which hitherto had been exercised by Government Ministers. These included delegated powers to make subsidiary legislation. The Assembly was given a general competence (short of legislation) in the prerogative fields of the arts, sport and culture; and the collective effect of transferring the statutory powers gave it wide authority to make executive decisions in some 17 subject areas. These included local government, education, health and social services, pollution, land use and development, transport, highways, road traffic, water and tourism.

51   The Assembly was to operate on local government lines. The powers were vested in the Assembly (a corporate body) as a whole, but the effective decisions as to their exercise would commonly have been taken by one of its committees or, where authorised, by the committee leader (or 'Executive Member'). Committees had to be established to cover all the subject areas for which the Assembly was responsible; their membership had to reflect the balance of the parties in the Assembly. The committee leaders, who could be supplemented by other Assembly members up to two thirds of their number, comprised an Executive Committee. Its chairman/leader would have been to all intents the senior Executive figure in the Assembly.

52   Powers transferred to the Assembly could no longer be exercised by Ministers, except where the Act permitted. A limited number of powers were made concurrent e.g. compulsory purchase of certain lands for the public service and the making of subsidiary legislation necessary to fulfil the UK's international obligations. But in general, Whitehall's interests were protected by other means:
- many of the powers were made subject to specific exclusions which maintained (or 'reserved') the existing powers of action in the Minister.
- the UK Government was authorised to intervene in the exercise of powers if they impinged on reserved powers by directing either that the action should not be taken, or certain action should be taken. These override powers could be used if the Secretary of State thought it "desirable in the public interest" or, in the case of subsidiary legislation, if it was considered to be incompatible with the UK's Community or international obligations.
- specific powers of intervention were conferred upon the UK Government, in the case of planning and water.
- the UK Government was authorised to give directions about the making of certain categories of subsidiary legislation affecting the National Health Service.

- the UK Government could issue guidelines to the Assembly about the exercise of its powers relating to industrial and economic functions of certain statutory bodies, including the Welsh Development Agency, the Land Authority for Wales and the Development Board for Rural Wales.

The 1978 Act as a Scheme for *Executive* Devolution

53   Given the premise that the most appropriate form of devolution for Wales was executive devolution, how useful is the Wales Act 1978 as a model? A further discussion follows in chapter 5 of alternative forms of executive devolution. This chapter focuses on the 1978 Act because it is likely to be the natural starting point for any Government wishing to revisit the subject.

54   The Act itself was drafted in the conventional form, no concession being made to the fact that it was, in essence, an organic law. It fails to describe the full range of functions that the Assembly was set up to perform. For example, no specific mention is made of its right to debate the Welsh perspective on matters currently being legislated by Parliament or other Welsh issues on which it had no powers to act, such as the relations of Wales with countries outside the United Kingdom. In essence, it merely enumerates the powers on which executive and delegated legislative action may be taken.

55   This mode of enumerating specific powers makes it difficult to gain a clear picture from the Act of what was being devolved and in particular what powers were reserved to central government. Those reserved powers are largely established residually, by working out what has *not* been devolved. What *actually* has been devolved can only be ascertained by examining the provisions of the legislation listed in the Act. The scheme is one which would have presented practical difficulties for those who had to work with the Act, and is likely to have been a source of uncertainty and interpretation disputes as the Assembly sought to formulate consistent policies over a general subject area.

56   The powers devolved and the exclusions are sometimes cast in less than immediately obvious language. They were the product of negotiations between the Welsh Office and the other concerned departments with little guidance on the principles that were to govern the selection of powers to be devolved. Whitehall departments such as the Treasury stoutly defended the need for national or economic consistency in their subject area. In consequence, many powers are subject to detailed qualification, which further obscures the principle behind the particular delegation. The result is an uneven picture between different subject areas; for some topics, the case for reservation appears weak e.g. building regulations. The Act gives the impression of being overly concerned to protect central authority, rather than seeking to confer sufficient competence on the Assembly to enable it to play an effective devolved role.

57   The decision to enumerate the devolved powers may have been, in part, a consequence of the Government's determination that the devolution statutes should not appear to create institutions with quasi-federal characteristics. Detailed identification of the powers to be transferred is the method used for executive decentralisation when powers are transferred from Whitehall to the Welsh Office by Order in Council under the Ministers of the Crown Act 1975. Conventionally, Ministers must be able to show legal authority for taking executive action. If the Assembly as a statutory body was to act in a particular subject area in place of Ministers, it could only do so

by taking over their powers as already enacted or by being given new powers, similarly particularised and circumscribed. As recasting the statute book was not a practical possibility, enumeration of the transferred powers was the logical consequence.

58   For all that it may be difficult to use, enumeration has the advantage of providing certainty as to what exactly has been transferred. In the last analysis, if the Assembly could point to an express power for a proposed course of action, it could proceed. Rather than criticise the mechanism, we might ask in retrospect whether a more relaxed attitude as to what could be devolved might have been adopted. In particular perhaps more opportunities could have been found for devolving all Ministerial powers under particular Acts, rather than under specific sections, and for fewer exclusions or specific reservations. In that event, other procedures for securing compatibility with national policies and interests might have had to be evolved, such as formal mechanisms for consultation and co-operation between the Assembly and Whitehall.

The 1978 Act as a Scheme for Devolution

59   The comments in the previous paragraphs rest upon the premise that the most appropriate scheme for devolution in Wales was executive devolution. But would it have worked satisfactorily? Would it have constituted a long-term constitutional solution?

60   A number of considerations suggest that the scheme of executive devolution might have proved restrictive and unsatisfactory. Although the Assembly was to be an elected and representative body, it was given a limited capacity to develop and implement effective *policies* in relation to the general subject matters on which it had specific powers.

61   This is evidenced in several ways. First, having no primary legislative power, it was expected to give effect to the legislative policy as enacted at Westminster. No mechanism was provided whereby the Assembly could ensure that its policy position would be taken into account in future primary legislation. The Assembly had no formal link with sponsoring departments in relation to legislative preparation; and no procedures were identified to facilitate the enactment by Parliament of amendments to existing Acts found by the Assembly to be restrictive.

62   Second, it was given no taxing power. At the best, it could have withheld a portion of the rate support grant (which would have been paid out of the block grant paid to the Assembly) to fund its own policies, thereby obliging local authorities to increase their rates in order to make good their shortfall. But generally, being dependent on a block grant, it could not be held electorally responsible for the way it sought to raise revenue in order to give effect to its policies. Further, since many of the activities funded out of the grant were likely to be carried out by local authorities under powers conferred directly upon them by primary legislation, the Assembly would have limited financial capacity to develop new policies for itself and to acquire the additional funding that it considered necessary. It would have been answerable only for spending on those matters upon which it enjoyed some financial leeway. To an extent, its spending priorities would have been dictated by the policies of central government embodied in primary legislation, which the Assembly had no power to influence.

63   Finally, the method of devolving detailed enumerated powers derived from statutes that had not been drafted with devolution in mind. Some Acts confer wider powers of discretion than others, even though they touch upon the same general subject matter. The Assembly's capacity to

develop a coherent policy in a subject area would have been dependent upon whether particularised powers had been devolved and would have been restricted by the divergences in the form of the powers devolved.   Similarly, the Assembly's power to make secondary legislation depended upon the nature of the powers devolved.   Again, the division between primary legislative provision and the conferment of delegated powers does not follow a consistent practice, one statute to another.   The ability of the Assembly to use its subsidiary law-making powers to develop coherent Welsh policies would have depended upon the extent to which particular Acts happened to delegate appropriate powers.

64   Although the Assembly was given a subordinate, executive role, it would have had claims, as an elected body, to special legitimacy in respect of the policy it developed.   Given the limitations just described, it would have had strong inclination, and usually some grounds, to attribute the responsibility to Westminster and Whitehall, whenever the Assembly was criticised for the way it carried out its functions.   So, it might have been expected, from early in its life, to press for extension of its powers to enable it to perform its functions more effectively, leading to potential conflict with central government if its requirements were not met.

65   Most importantly, every single piece of new Westminster legislation would have had to be considered, and drafted, with the needs of the devolved Assembly in mind, creating the potential for a continual re-run of the devolution argument.   The want of clearly-stated principles on what should or should not be devolved would have complicated that task.   Even in these respects, the Assembly had no formal role granted to it with respect to the formulation of the legislative policy for any new statute, or indeed, in respect of bills under consideration in Parliament.

66   In giving the Secretary of State override powers, the Act spelled out the criteria for their use in broad terms, creating yet another area of potential conflict.   It is a little surprising that central government took override powers with no formal provision for consultative procedures, when politically those powers were likely to be used only in the most exceptional and contentious circumstances.   By contrast, the intervention powers, which might have been expected to be invoked, or their use threatened, more readily than the override powers, did allow the Assembly's position to be formally taken into account, by the Assembly making formal representations.

67   The Act placed the office of Secretary of State in an anomalous position.   Indeed, it is not apparent that a separate office for Wales could have been justified after the transition was completed.   Might the remaining Welsh Office powers not have been reclaimed by the Whitehall departments, since many of the reserved matters had been made such because of their national dimension?   Was the Secretary of State's principal role to act as a go-between or to protect the interests of central government?   How could the Secretary of State have realistically spoken on Welsh issues in Cabinet and Parliament without the post having any formal link with the Assembly?   How effective would the office-holder have been if from a different party from that in power in the Assembly?

68   The scheme of subsidiary law-making might have had a number of undesirable consequences:

● by vesting the function of subsidiary law-making in the Assembly, the implementation of a legislative scheme ceased to be the responsibility of the department that sponsored the primary legislation.   This contradicts one of the major reasons for this form of law-making: to permit the authority that formulated the scheme to develop and adapt it to prevailing circumstances. The Assembly would have had to work within the limits set by a department without any formal capacity to influence the making of the original scheme, or to participate in the review and amendment of the scheme at a future date. This was not the case with respect to decentralised powers when exercised by the Welsh Office, which maintained a working link with the sponsoring department.

- no body of principles has been consistently applied in determining when and to what extent subsidiary law-making powers should be provided in a legislative scheme. The practice is very uneven between different Acts, even those concerned with the same general subject area. Decisions in the past about delegation, of course, did not take account of the needs under devolution. Would Parliament have recognised the need to produce consistent practice?

- the effects on the future form of delegated law-making powers are conjectural. But it is probable that wider and less constrained powers would have been considered necessary under new legislation if the Assembly were to enjoy a reasonably effective policy-making capacity. Would that have led to different, and broader, powers for the Assembly in comparison with those given to departments? Or is it more likely that the same broad powers would have been conferred on departments too, leading to even greater discretionary powers in central government than at present?

- much subsidiary legislation today is concerned with giving effect to European Community law, much more so than in 1978. The various override powers in the Act imply that Whitehall was reluctant at that time to see variations in implementation. This would have become an area of considerable tension between the Assembly and central government. Unless Whitehall would have been prepared to allow the Assembly to adopt alternative solutions, consistent with the European directives, the override powers here could have come into prominence.

69. The Act made no provision for consultative procedures on matters of this kind. It confirmed the status of the Assembly as a *delegate* and a fully *subordinate* executive authority. It is arguable that many of the shortcomings of the Act in providing a stable constitutional arrangement stem from that perception. Legally and constitutionally it was accurate to treat the Assembly as a fully subordinate body, but it ignored the legitimacy and authority which would flow to the Assembly from its democratic mandate.

Conclusion

70. The devolution debate in the 1970s contained a number of features which may recur in the 1990s:
   - the dominance of Scotland may preclude a proper debate in Wales, especially if the Welsh legislation is introduced in the same session as that for Scotland.
   - parliamentary opposition may come from the Government's own backbenchers.
   - key factors in the debate will be the cost of the Assembly and increase in bureaucracy; the impact on local government; and concern about the possible break-up of the UK.
   - there will be pressure in some quarters for a referendum.

71   The Wales Act 1978 gave little clear picture of what powers were being devolved and set out an excessively complex scheme. Given its starting point of executive devolution only, detailed enumeration of the transferred powers may have been unavoidable. It would have created an uneven patchwork of devolved powers, varying with the degree of discretion conferred by existing statutes (none drafted with devolution in mind); and future primary legislation for Wales might have had to be drawn more loosely than equivalent legislation for England. Executive devolution might not have been stable, might have increased the tensions between London and Cardiff, and might have proved to be an unsatisfactory transitional arrangement.

Chapter 3

Devolution in the 1990s

Introduction

72   ·The previous chapter suggested that the Wales Act 1978 may have been seriously flawed. Even if it is regarded as a sound model for its time, the world has moved on since the 1970s, particularly the world of government. The new Assembly will be operating in a very different political and administrative context. This chapter begins by describing the main changes that have taken place in the government of Wales since 1978, to give the new base line of institutions which the Assembly will control, and with which it will need to interact. The chapter then gives an account of the main arguments for and against devolution. It concludes by drawing these arguments together into a set of policy objectives which seeks to summarise the main objectives which have been advanced for an Assembly.

The Policy and Administrative Context in the 1990s

The Welsh Office

73   The Welsh Office is only 30 years old. The first Secretary of State for Wales was appointed in 1964, and began with 225 civil servants. The initial responsibilities of the new department were in the field of housing, local government, highways and water. Planning was added at an early date, and since then the department and its functions have continually grown, until in 1994-95 it had a staff of some 2,500.

74   By 1970 the Welsh Office had taken on responsibility for child care, health, and primary and secondary education. Responsibility for selective assistance to industry was transferred in the early 1970s. In 1978 significant responsibilities were transferred for agriculture and fisheries; and for ancient monuments and historic buildings.

75   The main changes since the 1970s have been the growth in the industrial and economic development functions; and in the transfer of further and higher education. Since 1992 the Maastricht reforms have led to further agricultural responsibilities coming to the Welsh Office. In the onward march of administrative devolution there is little more that could be transferred, except for the police and criminal justice responsibilities of the Home Office.

76   Relatively little primary legislation applies exclusively to Wales. In recent years there has been only the Local Government (Wales) Act 1994, which introduced the new unitary authorities; the Welsh Language Act 1993; and the legislation in 1975 and 1976 establishing the Welsh Development Agency and the Development Board for Rural Wales. Most of the Secretary of State's powers are based on more general legislation, supplemented where appropriate by secondary legislation to meet Welsh circumstances.

77   The chief areas where responsibility has not been devolved are economic policy and taxation, defence, foreign policy, such Home Office functions as police, prisons, probation and fire, the Lord Chancellor's responsibilities for civil law and the courts, and social security. Even in the fields where the Secretary of State does have responsibility, the scope for independence may be limited. Thus, in the case of industrial support, the Secretary of State is bound by the general UK structure of grants to industry and EU rules.

78   The division of functions between Whitehall, the Welsh Office and local government in Wales is shown schematically in the table below. It is crude and illustrative only: the headings are highly compressed, many subjects straddle more than one column, and the dotted lines are there to emphasise the overlap. The overlap extends not merely between Whitehall and the Welsh Office, but between the Welsh Office and local government.

Table 3   Division of Functions between Whitehall, the Welsh Office and Local Government

Whitehall	Whitehall and Welsh Office	Welsh Office	Local Government
Defence	Europe	Natural resources	Economic
National security	Agriculture	Economic	development
Foreign affairs	Industry and training	development	Roads
Economic policy	Employment	Roads and transport	Buses
Monetary policy	Environmental	Local government	Housing
Taxation	protection	Housing	Education
Transport		Education	Social services
Air and rail		Social services	Planning
Criminal law		Planning	Waste collection
Police		Health	and disposal
Prisons		Welsh language	Civil emergencies
Probation		Arts and culture	Museums and libraries
Fire			
Civil law			
Courts			
Social security			
Broadcasting			

79   The financial support for the Welsh Office is provided by block provision from the Treasury. This used to be negotiated like any other departmental budget; but since 1978 changes have been based upon the 'Barnett formula', which has divided any increases - or decreases - in territorial spending in the proportions 5:10:85 to Wales, Scotland and England. In 1992 the formula was revised to reflect Scotland's declining share of population, and since then has divided block funding in the proportions 5.12 (Wales), 9.06 (Scotland) and 85 (England). An £85 increase in comparable expenditure in England automatically feeds through into £5 extra for the Welsh block - and the converse for decreases in expenditure.

80   Within the Welsh block the Secretary of State decides on the distribution of resources to roads, health, housing and his other areas of responsibility. There may be variations between the different heads of expenditure between England and Wales, although these tend to be confined to the margins. The Secretary of State is also responsible for local government finance in Wales, including the operation of the council tax and non-domestic rates. Decisions on the level and distribution of central government support to local government are also the responsibility of the Secretary of State. The Secretary of State has never needed to use his rate capping powers.

81   Many day to day responsibilities are delegated to a range of public bodies with varying degrees of operational independence. The growth of quangos is described separately in paragraphs 89 to 93 below. There are also the health authorities and trusts established under NHS legislation; and a small number of executive agencies established under the Next Steps initiative. The 1995 Civil Service Yearbook records just two: CADW, responsible for conserving ancient monuments, and the Welsh Planning Inspectorate.

Local Government in Wales

82   In the 1970s, the devolution debate took place in the aftermath of a major local government reorganisation, following the establishment by the Local Government Act 1972 of a two-tier structure of eight county councils and 37 district councils. In the 1990s, there has just been a further major reorganisation, introduced by the Local Government (Wales) Act 1994, which abolished the two-tier structure with effect from April 1996. There are now 22 unitary authorities, ranging in size from Merthyr Tydfil with 60,000 people to Cardiff with just over 300,000. There are also some 700 town and community councils, an optional tier covering only parts of Wales.

83   The three-year review process by which the Welsh Office led the reorganisation focused almost exclusively on the structure of local government, and in particular on boundaries. The role, functions, financing and management of Welsh local authorities remain more or less intact; with the exception of Home Office services (police, fire, magistrates' courts, probation service and coroners) where local government has lost its marginal role. Attempts to use the review to stimulate a wider debate on the role and nature of local government, to promote community and town councils, or to stimulate changes in the internal management of local authorities fell largely on deaf ears.

84   More significant changes in Welsh local government have occurred *outside* the provisions of reorganisation. As in England, there has been a gradual erosion of local government functions. These include higher and further education which are now controlled by funding councils; provision for grant maintained schools, and the transfer of powers through local management of schools to school governing bodies; the creation of independent careers and inspection services; the promotion of housing associations in place of local authority housing departments; and the potential to establish housing trusts. On the other hand, some new responsibilities have been acquired, notably in economic development; community care where £125m has been transferred from the Department of Social Security to local authority social services departments; and trading standards. These changes have significantly changed the balance of local authority direct service delivery.

85   It remains to be seen what the net costs and savings from reorganisation will be. In 1995-96 the capital and revenue expenditure of Welsh local authorities totalled £3bn. Five years ago research suggested that their current expenditure was about 20% higher than that of English shire counties and districts[11]. This reflects both higher levels of need compared with English counterparts (e.g. higher unemployment, higher levels of ill-health) and also higher costs of service provision especially in sparsely populated areas. At the same time, Welsh local authorities' tax base is lower than in England. The combined effect of higher expenditure and a lower tax base is a significantly higher central government contribution to local authority expenditure in Wales: the local council tax provides only 14% of revenue expenditure.

86   Within local authorities, by far the largest element of revenue expenditure is education, which accounts for approximately 45% of the total. Personal social services, local environmental services and the police account for a further 35%[12]. In contrast, housing is by far the largest

element of local authorities' capital expenditure, at 43.7% of the total, with roads (17%) and 'other local services' (23%) being the only other substantial components[13].

87   One area of change which has been largely unobserved is the reduction in the number of councillors. The abolition of a tier of local government has reduced the number of local representatives from 1,976 to 1,273. Although a somewhat better level of representation than in England, the ratio of local councillors to electors is still much lower than that found elsewhere in Europe.

Privatisation

88   Privatisation has transformed the size and scale of the public sector. Most dramatic has been the decline of the coal industry, which has shrunk from 24,000 jobs in 1980 to just 1,000 jobs by 1995. In steel, telecommunications, gas, electricity and water together the current employment total of some 31,000 is at least 50% down on the pre-privatisation figure. It is estimated that local government has lost some 14,000 jobs since 1979, many following the introduction of compulsory competitive tendering and the resultant privatisation of public sector jobs.[14]

Quangos

89   One of the major features of the last 20 years has been the expansion of the functions, roles and number of quangos operating in Wales. Much of the Welsh Office's work is concerned with policy while the actual delivery of services is the responsibility of the local authorities, health authorities and quangos.

90   It has been estimated that by 1994-95 non-departmental public bodies (NDPBs) operating in Wales totalled over 200 and controlled a budget of £2.1bn, a third of all Welsh Office spending, and nearly as much as the combined expenditure of all Wales' local authorities.[15] In 1995 the Secretary of State for Wales was responsible for making appointments to some 175 public bodies: the full list is in Appendix B.

91   Both Labour and Conservative Governments have been responsible for creating quangos. The Wales Tourist Board, the Welsh Development Agency and the Development Board for Rural Wales were established by Labour Governments in the 1960s and 1970s. Their powers and remit have been increased by subsequent Conservative Governments, which have continued to create new quangos. These include S4C (1981), the Cardiff Bay Development Corporation (1987), the Welsh Language Board (1988), Tai Cymru - Housing for Wales (1989), and the Further Education and Higher Education Funding Councils for Wales (1992).

92   A number of these quangos have very significant budgets. The Cardiff Bay Development Corporation will receive an anticipated £250m during its ten year life span. Tai Cymru - Housing for Wales has an expenditure on social housing of approximately £200m a year. The Welsh Development Agency receives annual grant in aid of some £70m, and the Development Board for Rural Wales some £30m. Further details about these and other executive quangos are in Appendix A.

93   Since the Conservatives came to power the use of quangos has increased, as has the reaction against it in Wales. The standing of quangos has been hit by a number of public scandals; and the political complexion of the senior appointments to certain quangos has become a matter of concern.

Wales and Europe

94   When devolution was last attempted in the 1970s the UK had only just joined the Common Market (as it was then known). Since then the European Community has grown enormously in its scope, in the range of its activities, and in its impact on Welsh affairs. In fields like agriculture more legislation now comes from Europe than from Westminster. The Welsh Office has created (but since merged) its European Affairs Division; leading Welsh local authorities have teams of European liaison officers; and Welsh local government has joined with the Welsh Development Agency and other public bodies to open the Wales European Centre in Brussels. It is estimated that Wales receives around £100m a year from the European structural funds.

95   Following the Maastricht Treaty, the influence of the European Union will continue to increase; as will the interest in developing a 'Europe of the regions'. But the Committee of the Regions is still only a consultative body, and its three Welsh representatives are nominated by the Secretary of State. This serves as a reminder that it is the UK which is the member state, and Wales has no right of direct representation in the Council of Ministers. In agriculture, employment, consumer legislation, etc. the Whitehall departments lead, and Welsh interests are subsumed under UK interests.

Changes in the Health Service and in Education

96   The health service in Wales is run by the NHS Directorate at the Welsh Office, with an annual budget of just over £2bn. Since the 1970s the main change has been the introduction of the internal market in the NHS, with the division of functions between district health authorities and GP fundholders as purchasers and NHS Trusts as service providers. The NHS and Community Care Act 1990 established NHS Trusts as corporate bodies which would assume responsibility for the ownership and management of hospitals and other NHS facilities. They are run by boards of directors appointed by the Secretary of State. Starting in 1992, Trusts have been established in three successive waves, with 24 NHS Trusts established in Wales by December 1994. Trusts supply ambulance, community and mental health services as well as running hospitals. On the purchasing side, the nine DHAs and eight FHSAs are being merged into five purchasing authorities covering all of Wales.

97   In education the main change has been the Welsh Office assuming responsibility for further and higher education. In 1993, the 25 further education colleges and two sixth form colleges in Wales were transferred from local authority control to be funded by the Further Education Funding Council in Wales (1994-95 budget £160m). At the same time responsibility for funding universities and institutes of higher education switched to the Higher Education Funding Council in Wales (1994-95 budget £210m). At school level the main changes have been the introduction of the national curriculum supervised by the Curriculum Council for Wales; local management of schools; allowing schools to opt out of local authority control, with 15 grant maintained schools funded directly by the Welsh Office in 1994; and creation of the Inspectorate of Schools in Wales.

The New Pattern of Public Services

98   In a short introduction it is not possible to describe all the changes that have taken place in Welsh government since 1978. Their cumulative impact has been to transform the scale and nature of the public sector. Major public services (coal, steel, water, gas, electricity, telecommunications) have been privatised; blue collar and now white collar functions are subject to competitive tendering or market testing; housing, further and higher education and training taken from local authorities and given to quangos or the private sector.

99   The changes have not simply been structural. The drive for greater economy, efficiency and effectiveness has induced a change in attitude and in the culture of the public sector. There is greater emphasis on the needs of the customers and clients, reinforced by the Citizens Charter, with less room for cosy monopolies run in the interests of the staff. Performance is monitored and measured against league tables which make it easier to expose inefficient and substandard services.

100   At the same time the attempt to introduce market disciplines has lowered staff morale and led to a highly fragmented public sector which is confusing for clients and the general public. Quangos and public services may have benefited from their greater operational freedom, but democratic accountability has not. The challenge for any Assembly is to reintroduce stronger lines of accountability and democratic control while retaining the efficiency gains and more competitive attitudes of the 1980s and 1990s.

The Rationale for Devolution

101   Over the last 30 years a variety of arguments have been put forward for devolution. The second part of this chapter starts with an account of the main arguments for devolution, bringing in a wider all-UK perspective as well as the specific arguments presented in Wales[16]. There is then a separate section on the arguments against and the drawbacks of devolution. These arguments are then drawn together into a set of policy objectives which seek to summarise the main objectives expressed (or implied) by proponents of an Assembly, and to address the drawbacks.

102   The rationale for devolution springs from a variety of different arguments:
   - **distinct identity:** "The demand for Welsh democratic representation now stretches back more than three generations. It is largely the result of our having a distinctive society and culture. We are not better, nor worse than our neighbours, but different".[17] Historically, the demand has also been associated with the Welsh language movement, but preservation of the Welsh language is now recognised as a separate issue, to be addressed by separate policy initiatives. Wales is a multi-cultural, multi-lingual society, where a sense of Welshness and Welsh identity must embrace all those living in Wales, and cannot depend simply on language or ethnicity.
   - **political representation:** Wales has long had a distinct set of political values and allegiance. Originally a stronghold of Liberalism, during this century the majority allegiance has shifted to Labour. At the 1992 general election Labour won 27 out of the 38 parliamentary seats in Wales (with 50% of the total vote), the Conservatives won six seats (29% of the vote), Plaid Cymru 4 seats (9%) and the Liberal Democrats 1 seat (12%). The sense of political disenfranchisement has been sharpened by 17 years of Conservative Government at Westminster. For the fourth time in succession, the Welsh Office has been under the control of a Government and political party not elected by a majority of the people in Wales.
   - **Europe:** Wales will need a strong regional tier of government to maximise its influence over Brussels, to access EU structural funds, to participate more effectively in the Committee of the Regions, and to develop partnerships with other regions. Involvement with other regions has opened Welsh eyes to the wider possibilities: "The Welsh Office makes much of our developing relations with the four 'motor regions' of Europe - Lombardy, Catalunya, Baden-Württemburg and Rhône-Alpes. I do not deny that the growth of co-operation between Welsh businesses and firms in these regions is an excellent initiative. It is significant, however, that all these Regions have in common a democratically-elected government which pursues an industrial strategy tailored to the needs of the region."[18]

- **local government reorganisation:** from April 1996 the eight counties and 37 district councils in Wales have been replaced by a single tier of 22 unitary authorities. Some may be too small adequately to provide the full range of services. A regional tier may be necessary to fill the gap, and to provide co-ordination and support to the new unitary authorities.
- **strategic planning:** certain functions are generally regarded as being too big for local government, but too local for central government. These include strategic land use planning; transport; economic development; environmental control; waste management; tourism; sport; and culture.
- **economic development:** traditionally regional economic development has taken the form of capital grants to assist land reclamation, infrastructure and environmental improvements, and to attract foreign inward investment. Wales has been relatively successful in this; but in future the most effective regional development strategies will be those which succeed in forging an integrated approach to innovation, technology and training. Studies of successful regions in Europe show the importance of a strong networking culture, public-private sector collaboration, driven by a commonly shared innovation strategy and sense of national purpose which can only come from strong and respected political institutions.[19]
- **maintenance of the Union:** at the beginning of this century failure to deliver home rule led to the separation of Ireland from the United Kingdom. Faced again with separatist pressures, Westminster could meet some of the nationalist demands by a judicious measure of devolution which would help to hold the Union together.

103 Next, proponents argue that we already have a *de facto* regional tier of government in Wales, but one which is largely unelected and insufficiently open and accountable. The **Welsh Office** since its creation in 1965 has hugely expanded its range of functions. It now covers local government, education and training, arts and culture, housing and health, employment, agriculture, industry, transport, environment and economic development. It is responsible for the expenditure of £7bn a year, some 70% of total public expenditure in Wales. The only line of accountability lies through Welsh Office Ministers answerable to the Parliament in London. Administrative devolution now needs to be matched by political devolution. **Quangos and NDPBs** have significantly expanded in recent years, with expenditure in excess of £2bn a year. With the creation of unitary authorities, it is estimated there will be more quango appointees running Wales than elected local councillors. It has been said that in no other part of the UK is such a high proportion of public expenditure authorised by non-elected public bodies.[20]

104 Finally, proponents draw upon a critique of the UK's over-centralised system of government which goes back at least to the report of the Royal Commission on the Constitution in 1973. The growing complexity of social, environmental and economic problems requires tailor-made and locally designed solutions that will not emerge from a top-down approach. The expertise, detailed knowledge and commitment of regional actors must be incorporated into the policy-making process.

105 In their Memorandum of Dissent to the Royal Commission's report, Norman Crowther-Hunt and Professor Alan Peacock argued that:
Central government is overloaded which means:
- Ministers have insufficient time for strategic and policy planning.
- there is lack of co-ordination between different parts of the overlarge Whitehall machine.
- lack of close contact between Whitehall and regions/branches leads to failure of policy planning and policy implementation.

Parliament:

- is congested, sitting for longer than most legislatures but giving inadequate scrutiny to legislation.
- fails to call Ministers effectively to account.
- has become a rubber stamp for the executive.

106 These failings of Parliament were illustrated by the handling of the Local Government (Wales) Bill 1994 which paved the way for the recent local government reorganisation. Since 1907, Standing Order No 86 has allowed all Welsh MPs the right to participate in the Committee stage of "any public Bill relating exclusively to Wales". To get its Bill through the House the Government suspended Standing Order No 86 and nominated Conservative MPs representing English seats onto the Committee to give itself a majority. Of the 32 Opposition MPs sitting for Welsh seats, only 13 were allocated places on the Committee. They faced 15 Conservative MPs, a majority of whom represented English constituencies.[21]

The Drawbacks of Devolution

107 As with any major change there are advantages and disadvantages. Advocates of devolution need to be aware of the drawbacks, and where possible to adjust their implementation plans accordingly:

- while devolution can be used to meet demands for separatism, devolution could also add fuel to the separatist fire by establishing political institutions in which separatist forces might enjoy a stronger voice.
- devolution could lead to greater variation in standards of delivery of public services. The welfare state is predicated on uniformity of standards, and on uniform conditions of service. If uniformity is important in any service, the function should be retained at the centre. Devolution could be damaging to the cause of equity.
- devolution has a cost. As a minimum the Welsh Assembly will need to be housed and serviced, with salaries for its members and staff. Depending on its functions and the scale of its activities, it will also impose costs on other levels of government and public services in Wales, which are unlikely to be offset by consequential savings.
- devolution will expose the level of central government grant to the nations and regions, by bringing the annual negotiations with the Treasury out into the open and making them the subject of political conflict. Historically, Wales has received more than its per capita share of direct Government spending. This could be put at risk.
- there is a fear amongst the business community that a Welsh Assembly could lead to higher levels of taxation in Wales and tighter regulation, leading to an outflow of investment and jobs.
- removal of quango functions to the Assembly could lead to a loss of the specialist and business expertise represented on the quango boards.
- there will be greater danger of *immobilisme* through regional resistance to national policy: central government may find it more difficult to get agreement in principle and implementation in practice.
- there is the risk of greater complexity with three levels of government, and of a loss in accountability because of buck-passing between the different levels.
- many advocates of devolution state that the aim is to devolve the functions of central government, and not to encroach on the powers of local government. It may not be possible to ring fence the functions and responsibilities of local government. Some functions might be

more effectively performed at regional level; and if the devolved government in Wales distributes local authority block grant it will determine the spending priorities. In Northern Ireland, the spending decisions on education and housing gravitated upwards from the local authorities to Stormont by its use of specific grants; and in several European countries the development of regional government has been accompanied by an erosion in the responsibilities of local government.[22]

- creation of the Assembly may be used as the trigger for reviewing the recent local government reorganisation in Wales. Any further changes in the structure and functions of local government will create a further round of disruption.

- during the campaign preceding the 1979 referendum, fears were variously expressed that a Welsh Assembly would be dominated by South Wales and the Labour Party; or that it would become a vehicle for the Welsh language lobby.

108 Fears have also been expressed that, without proper safeguards, the Assembly could fall prey to the kind of municipal corruption which has characterised local government in parts of Wales.

Some Reflections on Devolution

109 The previous section presented the main arguments for and against devolution. The final section draws these arguments together into a set of policy objectives for a Welsh Assembly. Before setting out the policy objectives there follows a brief commentary on certain of the political and financial aspects.

Political Considerations

110 Proposals for a Welsh Assembly are being put forward at a time of profound disaffection with the political process generally, with political parties and with politicians. In part it is hoped that the Welsh Assembly will remedy that. But it will not do so if it replicates the worst features of Westminster and Whitehall, or the worst features of local politics in Wales. In some parts of Wales alienation from conventional politics stems as much from long years of one-party rule at the local level. In Scotland the Scottish Constitutional Convention has shown a determination to use the Scottish Parliament to build a fresh political culture and a new approach to politics. It is a gap that there is no equivalent broad-based civic movement in Wales.

111 The criteria for retaining functions at the centre include:
- the need to safeguard equal political rights for all citizens of the UK.
- the need to safeguard constitutional rights, the protection of minorities, integrity of the democratic process: Bill of Rights, electoral law, anti-discrimination legislation.
- competitiveness of the British economy: regulation of trade and industry.
- sound money, interest rates, credit, banking and insurance.
- integrity of all public agencies by audit and inspection.
- uniformity in delivery standards of certain services e.g. social security benefits.

112 Any system created must be workable and durable. It must be robust in handling conflict and capable of operating with Governments of opposite political complexions.

Financial Considerations

113 If devolution is principally concerned with the more effective administration of policies determined by central government, it may be appropriate for the devolved level of government to be financed by block grant. But if the intention is to give Welsh voters the power to make choices that differ from those in other parts of the UK, or that differ from the choices that would be made by central government, there is a strong case for assigning taxation powers. Otherwise the opportunity for the Welsh Government to make independent choices may be a fiction. And to ensure accountability when the Welsh Government chooses to set higher levels of spending, it is desirable that the additional revenue required to finance that extra spending should be raised from the people of Wales.

114 Even if the Assembly is dependent on block funding, the distribution of the block should be determined as much as possible by local democratic choice. Any funding system needs to:
- maximise the incentives for the devolved government to be responsible and efficient.
- maximise accountability to local voters for its spending decisons.
- minimise the potential for Whitehall or Westminster to dictate spending priorities.
- minimise the potential for one layer of government to pass the buck to others.

Policy Objectives in Establishing a Welsh Assembly

115 This section draws on the earlier sections to summarise a list of policy objectives which have been advanced for a devolved Government in Wales. These are as follows:

Accountability
- to make the Welsh Office and its services more directly accountable to the people of Wales.
- to improve accountability for the activities of quangos in Wales through more effective scrutiny and monitoring.
- for all public bodies and services, to ensure there are institutional and procedural safeguards which provide for consultation, openness and transparency.

Cultural, National and Political Identity
- to reflect the distinctive needs and cultural identities of the different language and other communities in Wales.
- to give a political voice to the people of Wales, and to give full expression to the diversity of political opinion within Wales.

Subsidiarity and Popular Support
- to ensure decisions are made as closely to the people affected as possible, and are responsive to local needs.
- to increase citizen participation, citizen support and citizens' feelings of responsibility for the institutions and workings of government.

Representation of Wales at Westminster and the European Union
- to ensure Wales continues to be represented effectively at Westminster.
- to give Wales a clear voice in the European Union.

Economy, Efficiency and Effectiveness
- to ensure the institutions of government in Wales are efficient and effective in form and function.
- to provide strategic direction and support for the new unitary authorities.
- to ensure effective co-ordination between the different levels of government: local, regional, national and supranational.
- to ensure that any changes are introduced and accomplished at minimum cost.

Wealth and Job Creation
- to provide a governmental and regulatory framework which supports a high level of prosperity and quality of life in Wales, through:
  - economic stability
  - competitive levels of taxation and incentives for investment
  - a regulatory burden no higher than in competing areas
  - speedy decision taking.

Maintenance of the Union
- to safeguard equal political rights for all citizens of the UK.
- to minimise points of conflict between Wales and Westminster, and to develop institutions which are capable of operating with Governments of opposite political complexions.
- to recognise that if equality and national uniformity of service are more important than responding to local needs and diversity, then the function should be retained at an all-UK level.

Conclusion

116 The scale and nature of the public sector in Wales has been transformed since the 1970s. The biggest change is the impact of Europe. In agriculture, industry and the environment more legislation now comes from Brussels than from Westminster. In Wales the main changes have included the privatisation of coal, steel and the major utilities; reorganisation of local government into 22 unitary authorities; and further administrative devolution to the Welsh Office. The public sector is more fragmented, with many executive functions devolved to quangos.

117 From contemporary debates on devolution, and the policy statements of the opposition parties, the main objectives for a Welsh Assembly appear to be:
- to make the Welsh Office and quangos more directly accountable.
- to reflect the distinctive needs and cultural identity of Wales.
- to remedy the democratic deficit which led to the introduction of the poll tax and changes in education and the NHS which had no support in Wales.
- to give Wales a strong and distinctive voice in Europe.
- to provide the new unitary authorities with strategic direction and support.

Chapter 4

Role and Functions of an Assembly

Introduction

118 The last chapter ended by summarising the main policy objectives which have been advanced for a Welsh Assembly. This chapter moves on to consider the role and functions of the Assembly, leading into a discussion as to how the Assembly might best be designed to carry out those functions. It is a precursor for the more detailed analysis in the next two chapters on the powers, structure and procedures of the Assembly.

119 It is not the place of this report to prioritise the policy objectives: where they come into conflict it is a matter of political choice which of the objectives should have priority. Very broadly the objectives can be said to fall into two main categories:

Democratic inputs

- political identity: giving a stronger political voice to the people of Wales.
- democratic scrutiny: calling the Welsh Office and public bodies to account.
- decentralisation: bringing decisions closer to the people they affect.

Functional outputs

- wealth creation: maintaining a high level of prosperity and quality of life.
- effectiveness: delivering high quality public services.
- strategic co-ordination: building effective partnerships with local government, Westminster and the EU.

It is the democratic objectives which have provided the main arguments for establishing an Assembly, and if one is created will be its motivating force. But it is by its performance in delivering the functional outputs that the Assembly will be judged, particularly by those who still feel ambivalent about the Assembly, or have yet to form a view.

120 This chapter will focus mainly on the democratic objectives, because that is how the new functions and structures of government in Wales will be determined. The classic functions of a democratic assembly are making laws; controlling government expenditure and taxation; and providing criticism, scrutiny and redress of grievances. These are considered in turn.

The Law Making Role

121 The central question here is whether the Assembly should have powers to pass primary legislation, or executive powers only. Should it have powers to make laws suitable for Welsh needs and circumstances; or should it have power merely to adapt laws made in Westminster to the needs of Wales? At present all legislation governing Wales is made by the Westminster Parliament. The Welsh Office then has discretion to adapt those laws to Welsh circumstances by means of delegated legislation, departmental circulars and administrative action.

Delegated Legislation

122 In recent years the degree of discretion to develop a separate policy in Wales has significantly increased. Modern statutes typically give wide powers to Ministers: the Education Reform Act 1988, for example, contained dozens of such powers. These powers have seldom been exercised differently in Wales from in England; but Welsh Office Ministers have shown a growing confidence to develop separate policies for Wales. Welsh policy on mental disability is quite

distinctive and widely envied in England. Another recent example is the bringing together in a single document, *PPG Wales,* of new planning guidelines after years when Wales simply followed England.

123 The volume of Welsh statutory instruments and administrative circulars suggests the potential to develop a significant degree of administrative discretion; but the subject matter of many of these documents suggests otherwise. In 1994 the Welsh Office issued 64 statutory instruments (SIs) and 82 circulars. Scores of SIs are Orders establishing individual NHS Trusts, prescribing Welsh forms and the like. They do not appear to offer much scope for policy variation. More promising are the administrative circulars, which offer guidance on educational and social policy: the majority come from the Schools Administration Division, Curriculum Division, and the Community Care Division. Yet even here many of the circulars are identical with the equivalent English circulars.

124 But it is mistaken to make a judgement on the scope for policy variation based on current Welsh Office practice. The question is not what the Welsh Office does now but what a Welsh Government could do with powers available under Westminster legislation following devolution. The Welsh Office does not do things differently, partly for lack of resources to devise different policies, partly for lack of desire in the context of a unitary Government. A separately elected Welsh Executive need not feel so inhibited.

Executive or Legislative Power

125 And yet, and yet ... a Welsh Government which wanted to develop distinctive policies for Wales might find limited room for manoeuvre if it had to pin its hopes on legislation passed at Westminster. A number of factors outlined in chapter 2 suggest that such reliance might prove unsatisfactory:
- the Welsh Assembly would be dependent upon the degree of discretion conferred by the Westminster Parliament. A well intentioned Westminster Parliament might confer broad delegated powers; a different Parliament (perhaps controlled by a different party) might leave no room for local discretion or choice. It might not even be a question of intent; in the existing statute book the degree of Ministerial discretion varies greatly from statute to statute.
- there would be no capacity to amend existing statutes except through the Westminster Parliament, which might have other priorities.
- schemes for future legislation would be prepared in Whitehall by officials who were no longer responsible for their administration in Wales, losing the clarity and unity of purpose which should bind together legislation and its implementation.
- although Westminster has a mechanism for considering specifically Welsh legislation, in the Welsh Grand Committee (for second reading) and a Welsh Standing Committee (for the committee stage), this can be by-passed. And when it is utilised the Government can pack the Welsh Standing Committee with non-Welsh MPs in order to ensure a majority to get its legislation through.

126 In reality what matters is who initiates the legislation. Under our parliamentary system of Government legislation is as much a function of the Executive as of Parliament. In their work on constitutional and administrative law, de Smith and Brazier acknowledge that, although law making is theoretically a function of Parliament, "legislation is primarily a function of Government...a very large majority of Government Bills, introduced into Parliament by Ministers, are passed into law substantially in their original form". [23] So long as legislative

power remains with Westminster the initiative remains with the British Cabinet Government, which controls the legislative programme and the content of individual items within the programme.

127   Given the tremendous pressure each year on the legislative programme, it is unlikely that the UK Government is going readily to insert additional items to accommodate the needs of a devolved administration in Wales. This is a further argument for the Welsh Assembly having primary legislative power: to get round the Westminster logjam. With executive devolution, Welsh bills would have to take their chance in the long queue of measures put forward by Whitehall departments each year, only one quarter of which finds space in Westminster's legislative programme. With legislative devolution, Welsh bills could find their own priority, in a legislative programme prepared by the Welsh Executive and presented to the Welsh Assembly.

128   How much legislative power could be devolved is considered in the next chapter. The point being made here is that the choice between executive and legislative devolution depends upon the degree of autonomy to be conferred upon the devolved government in Wales. If the principal purpose behind devolution is the more effective implementation of policies determined by central government, then executive devolution will suffice. But if the Assembly is to develop (or preserve) separate policies for Wales in local government, education or the NHS it will need legislative powers. Otherwise it will be dependent on the legislation passed at Westminster and prepared by Whitehall, where the Government will have a different agenda and other priorities.

129   An Assembly with executive powers only risks incurring the worst of both worlds. It would create high hopes in Wales of independent action which the Assembly might not be able to fulfil; but be a permanent supplicant in Whitehall, leading to continuing tension between London and Cardiff. The Secretary of State for Wales and the Leader of the Assembly would both claim to know what was best for Wales and would end up being political rivals rather than political partners, even when drawn from the same party. When drawn from opposition parties the institutional tension could be debilitating and destructive.

130   An executive Assembly might be liable also to have a more difficult relationship with local government in Wales. In looking for ways of extending its power, it might be tempted to draw functions up from local government - to centralise education and social services, highways and planning - all in the name of providing co-ordination and strategic support, and to intervene more in local government decision making.

131   So far we have presented mainly technical reasons why executive devolution would be difficult to operate. But it is impossible to ignore the political dimension, and the drive which will come from Scotland. Just as the creation of a Scottish Parliament will generate greater interest in an Assembly for Wales, so the powers of the Scottish Parliament may be held up as a paradigm for Wales.

132   For all these reasons - political and well as technical - executive devolution seems unlikely to be a satisfactory or durable solution. But because of the ambivalence in Wales about an Assembly, executive devolution may be a necessary first step to get the devolution process started. The next chapter therefore considers how the legislation might be drafted to confer executive devolution; and subsequent chapters contain references to executive devolution wherever relevant. But the remainder of the report focuses mainly on an Assembly with legislative power,

as a more satisfactory long term solution. Much of the argument and analysis in each chapter applies to both models; but wherever the conclusions differ, depending on whether an executive or legislative model is chosen, that is made clear in the text.

Giving Wales a Stronger Political Voice

133 The Assembly should certainly give Wales a stronger political voice. At present there is no representative body which can speak for the Welsh nation. Westminster has only one Welsh Day debate each session, and Welsh Office Ministers answer questions once every three weeks. In December 1995, the Government announced plans, following a similar announcement for Scotland, to breathe new life into the Welsh Grand Committee, which consists of all the Welsh MPs. The Committee has generally been regarded as a talking shop (and it has met just eight times in the last three years). In future, other Cabinet Ministers are to appear before the Grand Committee to answer questions on Welsh matters; there will be at least four meetings a year, with some held outside Cardiff; oral questions will be put to Welsh Office Ministers; and short debates and more substantial discussions will be held on Government policy.

134 Opposition MPs were quick to condemn the Government's proposals as 'a meaningless sop' and 'a tarted-up talking shop'. The difficulty in ensuring adequate accountability through Westminster was illustrated soon afterwards. A month after the Government's announcement, when Welsh Office Ministers next faced Questions in Parliament, of the first 24 Questions down for answer 16 had been put down by English MPs. This tactical manoeuvring may reflect the Government's weak parliamentary position in Wales; but Westminster's mechanisms of accountability will always remain vulnerable to pre-emption by English MPs. The Assembly should be capable of calling Wales' political leaders to account more frequently and effectively than this; and it will have far more opportunities to express the national mood, both in its day to day business and on set piece occasions. The publicity given to its proceedings should help enhance public interest in Welsh affairs, and educate and inform the public by the wider diffusion of facts, arguments and discussions of policy.

Control of Taxation and Expenditure

135 For maximum democratic accountability the Welsh Assembly should be responsible for raising the revenue to fund its own expenditure: whether this is feasible is considered in chapter 10. Here we will consider the Assembly's function in controlling the overall level and distribution of Government expenditure in Wales, and in monitoring its efficiency and effectiveness.

136 The Welsh Office is currently responsible for a budget of some £7bn a year. Local government in Wales receives just over £2bn of this. That budget will need to be debated each year to give the Assembly the opportunity to comment on its overall adequacy, and on the proposed distribution of the budget between the main heads of expenditure. For monitoring the efficiency and effectiveness of spending programmes, there will need to be a Public Accounts Committee, which to be effective will need to be serviced by a Welsh version or branch of the National Audit Office. Separate enquiries can be conducted by specialist scrutiny committees; again their effectiveness will be enhanced if their enquiries are based on audit reports.

Democratic Criticism, Scrutiny and Redress of Grievances

137 Chapter 6 concludes that the Assembly should not itself deliver services on the local government model, but should set the policy framework and call to account those who do deliver such services. The role of the Assembly will be to provide strong democratic control and oversight. It can scrutinise framework documents and discuss the key targets and performance measures for individual public services; and it can call the leaders of services to account if their performance is unsatisfactory. It can also seek to highlight particular concerns through question time sessions and Opposition Day debates.

138 Assemblies provide a forum for ventilating the grievances of individuals, localities and organised groups. Members may raise issues by asking questions, putting down motions, and raising constituency matters in debates. This is the stuff of politics for many local and national politicians. But there is a risk of the Assembly being diverted by parochial concerns: its committees and debates must be designed to address strategic and policy questions. And it must recognise that effective redress for injustices suffered by individuals is more likely to be achieved outside the Assembly, by members' letters and other representations, by referring complaints to the Ombudsman, and by using the machinery of tribunals and judicial review.

Conclusion

139 The classic role and functions of a democratic assembly are making laws; controlling government expenditure and taxation; and providing democratic scrutiny.

140 The Liberal Democrats and Plaid Cymru both propose a Senedd with law making powers. Labour's Assembly would have powers of secondary legislation, which would vary with the degree of discretion conferred by statutes passed at Westminster. If the Assembly is to develop (or preserve) separate policies for Wales in local government, education or the NHS it will need legislative powers. Otherwise it will be dependent on the legislation passed at Westminster and prepared by Whitehall, where the Government may have a different agenda and other priorities.

141 The Assembly should also be able to call Welsh political leaders to account more frequently and effectively than does Westminster.

Chapter 5

The Powers of the Assembly

Introduction

142 The previous chapter explained the difference between executive and legislative devolution, and the limitations on the autonomy of the Assembly if the model chosen is one of executive devolution only. This chapter considers how the legislation might be framed in order to confer executive or legislative powers; and explores ways around the difficulties thrown up in the Scotland and Wales Acts of 1978. It looks first at executive devolution; then at limited devolution of legislative power; and then at legislative devolution covering all Welsh Office subjects.

143 Executive power needs separate consideration because the Assembly may be created with executive powers only. But even with legislative devolution there needs to be separate transfer of the executive powers of government. There may also be a difference in extent between the executive and legislative powers devolved: in 1978 the executive powers devolved to Scotland went wider than the legislative powers of the Scottish Assembly.

Executive Devolution

144 For a scheme of executive devolution only there are essentially two models: that adopted in the Wales Act 1978, based upon the detailed transfer of statutory powers; and the broader approach adopted in the Government of Ireland Act 1920. When the Welsh Office was created and subsequently expanded, functions were transferred from Whitehall by means of detailed lists of powers in a series of Orders in Council made under section 1 of the Ministers of the Crown Act 1975 (and its predecessor Act). In some cases all the executive powers under a particular statute were transferred; in others all powers except under specified sections; in yet others only powers under particular sections or even sub-sections.

145 The Wales Act 1978 followed a similar pattern. If this technique were adopted in a future Wales Bill, the schedules might be less convoluted if the settlement were less grudging. There might then be more cases when all the powers under individual statutes could be devolved. But the task of formulating the list would remain formidable. The end product would still remain daunting, and of little immediate guidance as to the nature of the powers devolved.

146 The Government of Ireland Act 1920 which established the Stormont Parliament adopted a different approach. Delegation was effected not by specific itemisation of powers but in the Letters Patent to the Governor who was authorised to do all that the Lord Lieutenant of Ireland had customarily been entitled to do before 1922. The Executive could use any statutory powers so long as they did not arise out of legislation on a reserved matter. This was made easier by the fact that Stormont by its own legislation could, if it wished, amend or replace existing executive powers derived from UK Acts.

147 Could this approach be adopted for a Welsh Assembly? In principle the transfer could be made in broad terms as covering all the executive powers which prior to devolution were exercisable by the Secretary of State for Wales. The existence of powers would be determined as at present by looking at the statute book and the transfer orders and by substituting the devolved Government for the Secretary of State. A similar approach has been adopted by the draftsmen

when creating new courts such as the High Court in 1873 or the Crown Court in 1971: they were simply declared to have inherited the jurisdiction of their predecessors. But this device would have the disadvantage of giving no indication in the bill of the general competence of the Welsh institutions. That might be overcome by categorising in the bill the broad subject areas but indicating that the only powers that could be used were those hitherto vested in the Secretary of State or subsequently transferred by or under an Act of Parliament.

Limited Devolution of Legislative Powers

148 There are few historical precedents for very limited legislative devolution. It might arise in two possible contexts: if there was a wish to transfer legislative powers in stages; and if there was a wish to implement the policy proposed in the Labour Party's policy document *Shaping the Vision* (May 1995) of the Assembly having limited legislative power to restructure quangos and local government.

Phased Devolution

149 The legislative model for devolution in phases is to be found in the Northern Ireland Constitution Act 1973. It offered the basis for a gradualist approach by requiring legislative and executive powers to be treated under three heads:
   - **transferred matters:** matters transferred to the Assembly and Executive by Order in Council laid before Parliament by the Secretary of State - section 2 (1).
   - **reserved matters:** matters that were not initially transferred, but could be transferred at a later date - section 3(1).
   - **excepted matters:** matters that could never be transferred - section 2(2)(a).

150 The 1973 Act was not implemented, so it is not possible to illustrate which matters were transferred at the outset, and which subsequently. It nevertheless shows how a scheme of phased devolution might operate, with parliamentary checks (but without the need for primary legislation) at each subsequent transfer of power. The range of powers transferred initially would be a matter of choice. One possibility would be to follow the historical pattern of gradual transfer of responsibilities to the Welsh Office over the last 30 years, starting with local government, housing, Welsh language, arts and culture. The legislative responsibilities of the new Assembly could gradually be extended to education, health, social services, etc. as confidence developed and the new Government and Assembly felt confident to legislate in these wider fields. There could be awkwardness if (for example) the Welsh Assembly had legislative responsibility for local government but Westminster was still responsible for housing, which suggests legislative power might need to be transferred in quite large blocks.

151 A major disadvantage of phased devolution is that because the Orders in Council would define the legislative powers *transferred* at each stage, it would have to follow the conceptual structure of the Scotland Act 1978, rather than defining the powers retained as did the Government of Ireland Act of 1920. The distinction is explained in paragraphs 176 to 180 below.

Devolution of Specific Legislative Powers

152   The Labour Party's policy document *Shaping the Vision*, though coming out against general powers of primary legislation, recognised:

> "*a need for some specified powers to be devolved to enable the Assembly to discharge functions which have otherwise been devolved to it in relation to the restructuring of quangos, the Welsh language and local government re-organisation*".

The Assembly would need legislative power to restructure quangos or local government or to alter Welsh language provision. This could be transferred in the form of power to make primary or delegated legislation.

153   In principle, the Assembly could be given the legislative powers necessary to make Acts of its own on these topics including the power to amend and repeal existing Acts of Parliament. But they could sit awkwardly with an executive body. For example, appropriate Assembly procedures for enacting the legislation would be needed which, after their initial use, might rarely be required. The bill would have to make provision for matters which were unlikely to arise: reserve powers in favour of Parliament, special safeguards in respect of EU or other international obligations, override powers, provision to resolve conflicts of legislative competence.

154   An executive Assembly would have powers, and well worked procedures and safeguards to make delegated legislation on a wide range of specific issues. Extension of its powers to enable it to make delegated legislation on these broad topics would be feasible; but it would need to be in sufficiently wide or detailed terms and to authorise amendment of existing Acts of Parliament. Framework legislation (which leaves the delegate, rather than Parliament, to decide on the policy) and 'Henry VIII clauses' (which allow the delegate rather than Parliament to decide to amend or repeal Acts) are not usually well regarded. But the arguments against are weaker when the delegate is an elected body.

155   Neither solution is particularly attractive. The solution most consistent with the rest of a scheme for executive devolution would be to confer delegated powers to legislate in the specific fields by rather broadly drafted provisions in the Wales Bill. There would need to be safeguards to ensure the broadly drafted provisions were not exceeded or abused, of the kind policed by the Joint Committee on Statutory Instruments when it scrutinises secondary legislation. There could also be a requirement that the delegated legislation be subject to confirmation by the UK Parliament.

156   Adoption of either solution is an implicit concession that if it is to take major policy initiatives the Assembly will need general legislative powers. It underlines the argument that, without such powers, the Assembly would be restricted in its ability to develop distinctive policies of its own, and would be dependent on the UK Parliament to legislate on its behalf.

Legislative Devolution

157   The remainder of the chapter considers a fuller scheme of legislative devolution, as advocated by the Liberal Democrats, Plaid Cymru, the Parliament for Wales Campaign and Welsh Labour Action.[24] It begins by explaining how legislative devolution would operate within the continuing sovereignty of the Westminster Parliament, and then considers which powers might

be devolved; whether the legislation should recognise shared powers; and whether the legislation should define the powers devolved to Wales or the powers retained at Westminster. It concludes with ways of making the legislation more flexible than in 1978.

The Continuing Supremacy of Parliament

158 It is important to state at the outset the continuing primacy of Westminster. That is the underlying basis of legislative devolution within the UK; and it should enable greater flexibility in the settlement, because it means that *even on devolved subjects* Westminster can if it wishes continue to legislate. It would not wish to do so frequently or needlessly, for that would undermine the whole basis of the settlement; but Parliament can devolve legislative power secure in the knowledge that when the need arises its will can prevail. That was the constitutional relationship between Westminster and Stormont, reserved by section 75 of the Government of Ireland Act 1920 which provided:

> *"Notwithstanding the establishment of the Parliament of...Northern Ireland...or anything contained in this Act, the supreme authority of the Parliament of the United Kingdom shall remain unaffected and undiminished over all persons, matters, and things in Ireland and every part thereof."*

159 This preservation of Parliamentary sovereignty extended to the delegation of legislative power, and the effect has been described by Professor Harry Calvert as follows:

> *"There have been cases where Westminster legislation within the sphere of transferred matters has extended to Northern Ireland, but it has always been with the consent of the Northern Ireland government, sometimes willingly, sometimes without great enthusiasm on their part. There have also been occasions when interference was threatened failing the taking of legislative action on the part of Northern Ireland by its parliament and legislative action has consequently been taken, even with great reluctance."*[25]

160 Under the Government of Ireland Act 1920 there thus developed a convention of non-interference, but a recognition that *in extremis* Westminster could prevail. The same would hold in the case of any scheme of legislative devolution in Wales.

161 Against this background it is odd that the 1978 devolution legislation did not follow the 1920 model. Reference here is to the Scotland Act 1978 rather than the Wales Act, because the Scotland Act provided for a scheme of legislative devolution. It suffered from many of the same defects as the Wales Act which were identified in chapter 2:

- it attempted valiantly to divide all powers into watertight compartments, and to eliminate areas of overlapping responsibility. Concurrent powers were kept to an absolute minimum.
- in striving for certainty it specified in extreme detail the powers devolved, and in equal detail the excepted powers to be retained, in schedules running to dozens of pages of incomprehensible legislation by reference.
- there was very little allowance for Scotland to stray onto the territory of Westminster, and no capacity to amend the schedules except by further primary legislation.

162 In short the 1978 legislation set out a rigid, over-specific and highly inflexible scheme. What follows may err too much in the opposite direction. In part this is because there is not time or space to work out the detail in all the different subject areas; but in part it is because we believe an excessively detailed approach is unnecessary and misconceived. In other countries

devolution legislation would be recognised as an organic law and drafted accordingly, in broad terms, so that it is comprehensible to anyone who reads it, and allows room for growth and development. That was the approach adopted in the 1920 Act; and (suitably updated) that should be the approach of any future devolution legislation.

163   The main changes since 1920 are the great extension in government activity, with the growth of the welfare and the regulatory state; and the similar extension at international and supra-national levels. Any new devolution legislation must recognise that with modern government, responsibility in many policy areas is shared between a number of different levels - European, national, regional and local. Where that is the case we have acknowledged the fact by proposing that the power be shared, rather than by trying to divide it up into separate compartments, demarcated for all time.

164   Legislation drawn in this way will not give total guidance as to who does what: in shared fields that is something that must be decided by political negotiation between the different levels of government, depending upon their legal obligations, political concerns and budgetary pressures - some of which will change over time. That is in effect what happens now in all the fields of EC competence; and in cases of conflict European law prevails. So here negotiations in fields of shared competence will not take place in a legal vacuum: in any given field Westminster if it chooses can prevail.

Powers to be Devolved

165   It is convenient to take as a starting point the principle adopted in Scotland by the Scottish Constitutional Convention, that legislative power could be devolved in all the subject areas currently the responsibility of the Scottish Office - in this case, the Welsh Office. But among these subjects there are some areas where Westminster would need to retain a degree of legislative responsibility, for three main reasons:

- **impact on the rest of the UK:** examples might include environmental impact e.g. lower pollution standards in Wales could adversely affect adjoining parts of England; economic impact e.g. ensuring a level playing field and fair competition between the different parts of the UK; or collective security e.g. denying planning permission for defence establishments.
- **enforcement of international obligations:** agriculture, industrial policy, environmental protection are now largely governed by European legislation: the UK Government must retain sufficient power to ensure that UK obligations to the EU are met. It must also ensure compliance with the requirements of the European Convention on Human Rights and other international law obligations.
- **harmonisation within a single legal system:** unlike Scotland and Northern Ireland, England and Wales are a single legal system. Conferring separate legislative power should not be allowed to distort the integrity of the underlying body of civil and criminal law: company law, commercial law, property law, etc. The Welsh Assembly may often accept or request uniform legislation by Westminster in order to maintain the common legal system.

166   These factors make it difficult to divide legislative powers into neat categories, because the need for legislation by Westminster will vary greatly from subject to subject. At one extreme it is hard to envisage Westminster needing to encroach on Welsh language legislation, or the preservation of Welsh ancient monuments and buildings; while in fields like transport or environmental protection the need for Westminster legislation may be relatively frequent. It is

not too difficult - save at the margins - to define the core of powers that need to be reserved, where Wales will have no legislative competence (list A in **Table 4** below). What is difficult is to decide whether to draw a distinction between those devolved subjects where Westminster may need to intervene frequently, and those where intervention will be a rare event, and may be regarded as a hostile act.

167 The constitutions of federal systems have had to face the same dilemma. Some, such as the Canadian constitution, divide powers simply into two categories, of those retained and those transferred. More commonly, however, federations, while conferring exclusive powers on the centre or the states, or even both, recognise a substantial category of concurrent powers. These include: Australia, Germany, India and Malaysia. In addition to listing these powers, federal constitutions generally indicate whether the residuary powers (i.e. those not specifically listed) are to rest with the centre or the states.

168 The policy should be to develop a distinction between those subjects clearly belonging to the Assembly, where Westminster interventions should be rare; and those subjects where Westminster interventions would be regarded as legitimate and welcome. In a federal system this would generally be achieved by dividing legislative powers into three categories: those reserved to Westminster (list A); devolved to the Welsh Assembly (list C); and those fields where legislative power may be exercised concurrently (list B).

Table 4 Division of Powers in a Federal System

A Reserved Powers	B Concurrent Powers	C Devolved Powers
Defence	Transport and highways	Welsh language
Foreign affairs	Agriculture, forestry and	Local government
National security	fisheries	Health and social services
Monetary/fiscal policy	Industry	Housing
Taxation	Economic development	Arts, culture, sport and tourism
Trade and commerce	Education and training	Ancient monuments and
Shipping	Environmental protection	historic buildings
Aviation	Land use planning	
Social security		
Elections *		
Bill of rights *		
Audit *		
Ombudsman *		
Civil and criminal law		
Courts		
Police		
Prisons		

Note: The items in italics are discussed in paragraphs 181 to 183 below

169   However in the British system Westminster would have the capacity to legislate even in devolved subject areas, so there may be no need for explicit recognition of concurrent powers, but simply a list of powers reserved and powers devolved:

Table 5 Division of Powers under Parliamentary Sovereignty	
A Reserved Powers	**B Devolved Powers**
Defence	Transport and highways
Foreign affairs	Agriculture, forestry and fisheries
National security	Industry
Monetary/fiscal policy	Economic development
Taxation	Environmental protection
Trade and commerce	Land use planning
Shipping	Welsh language
Aviation	Local government
Social security	Health and social services
*Elections**	Housing
*Bill of rights**	Education and training
*Audit**	Arts, culture, sport and tourism
*Ombudsman**	Ancient monuments and historic buildings
Civil and criminal law	
Courts	
Police	
Prisons	

Note: The items in italics are discussed in paragraphs 181 to 183 below

170   A listing of concurrent powers could be no more than a statement of powers in respect of which the UK Parliament was more likely, in contrast with the transferred powers, to legislate because of national considerations. But in our system legislation cannot lay down enforceable statutory rules as to how Parliament might exercise its legislative powers in future. The best that can be hoped for is that the circumstances in which Parliament would intervene (e.g. as mentioned in paragraph 165) could be covered by constitutional undertakings and practice that in due time might harden into a series of constitutional conventions.

172   If this sounds optimistic, it is important to reiterate two points: that the legislation needs to allow for interventions by Westminster, because of the overlapping responsibilities of different levels of government; and that legislative competence has been successfully shared in the UK (in the case of Stormont) and in other jurisdictions, notably those federal jurisdictions which recognise concurrent powers. There is also shared legislative competence between the EU and Westminster.

173   What is now required is a means of sharing legislative power between Westminster and Wales. One way would be for UK national legislation giving effect, for example, to European requirements to set the policy and financial framework, and the Welsh Assembly and Executive could prescribe more detailed standards and deliver the service. This would parallel the

mechanisms employed in Article 75 of the German constitution, which authorises the federal government to legislate skeleton provisions on higher education, regional planning etc, leaving the detailed legislation to the Länder.

174 What would be optimistic would be to place too much reliance on the principle of subsidiarity, which is not the magic key that some have suggested. The principle in its present state of development gives little guidance and could lead in effect to asking the courts to determine what should or should not be devolved: a responsibility which the courts would be unlikely to accept, and which would be unlikely to survive legislative scrutiny in the House of Lords. It is but one principle among a number which will guide the political negotiations between Whitehall and Wales about who legislates on what. These negotiations will not take place in a legal vacuum: in any given field Westminster, if it chooses, can prevail. Whether it chooses to prevail will depend upon the conventions which develop and on the political circumstances, resources and legislative time available. Although in theory Westminster could retain total control, in many fields it may find it convenient to devolve significant amounts of legislative power and budgetary responsibility.

175 There are also likely to be instances where the Welsh Assembly will request Parliament to legislate for Wales even in a devolved subject area. This may be particularly appropriate in fields where uniformity is desirable because of the unitary legal system, or in order to maintain uniformity of professional standards or service provision. Little is to be gained by requiring the Welsh Assembly to enact the same legislation: in terms of time, legislative priorities and possible loss of uniformity, there is much to be said in favour of Westminster carrying out such tasks. In such circumstances the initiative might be expressed to be with the Assembly to request the UK Parliament to legislate for Wales as well as for England.

Should the Legislation Define the Powers Devolved or the Powers Retained?

176 We have already discussed the merits of the Government of Ireland Act 1920 as a model for devolving legislative power rather than the Scotland Act 1978. The main difference was that the 1978 legislation was excessively rigid and compartmentalised, with no margin of flexibility. A second design question which needs to be addressed is whether the legislation should specify the powers reserved to Westminster, as in 1920, or the powers devolved to the new Assembly, as in 1978.

177 It is not necessary in such legislation to define both list A and list B: most constitutions define one set of powers or the other. Here too the federal systems offer alternative models. Some constitutions, such as the Australian, define the powers reserved to the centre, leaving the unspecified remainder to the states; others, such as the Canadian, define the powers of the provinces, leaving the remainder to be held by the centre. The remainder may be large or small, depending on the length of the counterpart list; it will also include residuary powers over subjects not yet thought of.

178 It is probably easier to define the powers retained at the centre (list A in the tables above). It requires less detail and specificity, as the draftsmen of the Scotland Act 1978 discovered. It may also provide for an easier passage in Parliament: parliamentarians may feel on surer ground defining the matters which should continue to be their responsibility at Westminster, rather than defining the powers devolved. This points towards legislation constructed on the 1920 model, with the Welsh Assembly being given power to make laws for the peace, order and good government of Wales, except in those matters reserved for Westminster.

179   The disadvantage with such an approach is that the residuary powers would then be left with Wales. Examples of residuary powers from the Canadian constitution of 1867 would be aviation and wireless telegraphy, subjects not then on the map of governmental responsibilities. Caution suggests that such unknown powers should be left with the centre. That was one of the factors which motivated both the Royal Commission on the Constitution and the framers of the 1978 Act to define the powers to be devolved, so that the remainder should be left with Westminster. It would also make clear to the people of Wales what was being devolved if the legislation set out the main subjects over which the Assembly would have legislative power. But given the overriding sovereignty of Parliament the 1970s concern about residuary powers was overdone. Westminster can intervene to reclaim residuary powers which acquire national significance, and concern about residuary powers alone should not determine the design of the legislation.

180   Before leaving this subject we should also deal with the common misconception that because the Stormont Parliament failed its constituent legislation does not offer a good precedent to follow. Most commentators agree that as a model of devolution the Stormont legislation worked reasonably well, albeit within circumstances where the Unionists did not want to rock the Westminster boat. The political breakdown in Northern Ireland came because the Unionists abused their dominant position. The 1920 model could certainly work for Wales; but (mindful of Northern Ireland) with checks and balances to prevent domination by one political party. The main checks suggested in this report are that there should be separation between the Executive and the Assembly (discussed in the next chapter); that the Assembly could be elected by PR (chapter 11); and that it should not have power on its own to change the electoral system (discussed below). The rights of minorities could also be protected by a Bill of Rights.

Electoral System, Bill of Rights, Watchdog Bodies

181   None of the lists in Tables 4 and 5 is sufficiently detailed as it stands for inclusion in legislation, and there is room for argument about the categorisation of certain subjects. The electoral system, Bill of Rights and arrangements for audit and other watchdog functions merit separate discussion. A Welsh Assembly with legislative powers would be responsible for local government in Wales, including its electoral arrangements; and it could be left responsible for deciding its own electoral system. However it is salutary to remember the history of Stormont, which when created in 1922 was established on the basis of proportional representation. A few years later the Unionist Government changed the electoral system to 'first past the post'. Wales has a similar history of one party domination (and for the same period, with the Labour Party's dominance dating from 1922). It seems undesirable to leave the choice of electoral system to the locally dominant party. Perhaps mindful of this, the Scotland Act 1978 left the electoral arrangements for the Scottish Assembly with the Secretary of State. That may tilt the balance too much the other way. The best solution might be to create a 'dual lock', permitting the Assembly to make changes to the electoral system, but requiring the assent of Westminster before it does so. A further safeguard could be to require a 'triple lock', putting any major change in the franchise or electoral system to the people of Wales in a referendum.

182   In the UK, discussion of a Bill of Rights focuses on two main options: incorporation of the European Convention on Human Rights into national law; or the development of a home grown Bill of Rights. The ECHR has been ratified by the UK and both the Labour Party and the Liberal Democrats are committed to its early incorporation as a first step in the development of a domestic Bill of Rights. There is considerable logic in the ECHR being incorporated into UK law,

because it involves observance of the UK's international obligations and would provide a minimum standard of human rights law across the UK. The development of a domestic Bill of Rights might also be thought more appropriate to Westminster, but need not necessarily be so. There has for a while been interest in Northern Ireland in adopting its own Bill of Rights; and the Scottish Constitutional Convention has declared that a Scottish Parliament should be responsible for developing a Scottish Bill of Rights encompassing social and economic rights as well as the more traditional civil and political rights. Individual nations within the UK should not be discouraged from adopting higher human rights standards than the minimum laid down in the ECHR; the question is whether uniformity of these higher standards across the UK is desirable. A Welsh Bill of Rights might seek to outlaw discrimination against particular minorities in Wales - political and linguistic minorities being two possible groups who might need such protection.

183   The watchdog functions comprise audit (the National Audit Office and the Audit Commission), ombudsmen (the Parliamentary Commissioner for Administration, the Health Service Commissioner and the Commissioners for Local Administration), the Public Appointments Commissioner and the Boundary Commission. Different considerations apply in each case. Ombudsmen are normally officers of Parliament, and the Welsh Assembly should have its own Ombudsman to investigate complaints against the Welsh Executive and perhaps other public services in Wales. In the field of audit, the National Audit Office will be auditing most Government expenditure in Wales anyway, because of its responsibility to trace central government funds. It already does work under contract for various other bodies. It could report to Parliament for central government expenditure and to the Assembly on Welsh Government expenditure; or a separate Audit Office could be created in Wales (the Wales Act 1978 created a separate Welsh Comptroller and Auditor General). In the case of public appointments Wales will probably want its own guardian; but it could start by inviting the Public Appointments Commissioner at Westminster to continue scrutinising appointments in Wales on behalf of the Assembly. All these bodies need a minimum caseload to enable them to function effectively; one way to build up a sufficient case load is to combine more than one function in the same office holder - the Parliamentary Commissioner in Northern Ireland, for example, also covers local government.

Other Ways of Building in Flexibility

184   Overall little advantage was taken in the 1978 legislation, in dealing with potential disputes as to jurisdiction, of the fact that the schemes involved *devolved* powers, under which ultimate authority remains with the central authorities, in particular the UK Parliament. In principle, this should permit a more flexible approach to be taken when matters arise in which central and devolved authorities both have an interest.

185   The final part of this chapter sets out possible 'expansion joints' and points of flexibility which would make it easier to draft the legislation in broad terms and also to devolve matters which otherwise might be reserved. The essence is that the legislation should be capable of adaptation to changing circumstances, and should allow either Government to trespass on the territory of the other. Because the 1978 legislation largely failed to provide for this, it may be helpful to spell out the techniques by which such flexibility might be achieved.

Authorised Trespass

186 Federal constitutions on occasion expressly authorise the federal parliament to extend the States' powers to legislate to matters on the federal list[26]. The Scotland Act permitted limited legislative action with respect to matters outside the Assembly's competence if they were "merely incidental to or consequential on" devolved matters on which it was legislating.

187 It should be possible to go wider than this, by prescribing in the devolution legislation a procedure under which the Assembly could be authorised to deal with a particular issue not within its competence, by Order in Council subject to parliamentary disallowance. This need not be limited to ancillary matters. In effect this could be used as a form of particularised devolution following agreement between the central and devolved authorities.

Requested Legislation

188 Under a devolved scheme, the UK Parliament would continue to legislate for Wales on reserved matters. In principle, then, it could respond to a formal request made by the Assembly to enact such legislation. The 1978 Acts made no reference to this aspect, since they were concerned with setting the limits to the Assemblies' competence. New devolution legislation could usefully recognise the competence of the Assembly to debate matters that are not within its legislative competence, and to pass resolutions including requests for Parliament to legislate.

Devolved Executive Powers

189 There are likely to be cases for which Parliament wishes to retain the legislative authority for both England and Wales, yet the administration of that legislation could be devolved. This is more likely to arise in a single legal system than, for example, in respect of Scotland. Examples might include Home Office subjects such as the police, probation, or fire service which might be the subject of executive but not legislative devolution.

190 The Scotland Act, section 63(3) and Schedule 11, identified a large number of existing powers devolved to the Scottish Executive under legislation not within the Assembly's competence, their exercise to be funded from the block grant. But no provision was made for changes to the list (nor for financial adjustments following the addition of powers). Nor was allowance made for the limited devolution of executive powers for particular occasions. To meet these cases, a Welsh devolution bill could expressly authorise devolution of specific executive powers - whether under existing or subsequent legislation - to the Welsh Executive by Order in Council, although the legislative authority on the matter was retained by the UK Parliament.

Conclusion

191 Executive devolution could be implemented by following the model in the Wales Act 1978, of listing in exhaustive detail all the statutory powers transferred; or it could transfer all the executive powers which prior to devolution were exercisable by the Secretary of State for Wales. Neither method would give a very clear indication to the public of the powers transferred.

192 If desired this could be coupled with limited legislative power. Legislative power could be transferred in stages; or for specific topics the Assembly's power to make delegated legislation could include a power to amend specified Acts of the UK Parliament. This would need safeguards and such delegated legislation might require confirmation by Westminster.

193 Legislative devolution for Wales should not follow the model of the Scotland Act 1978, which was too rigid and over specific. It should be drafted in broader terms and define the legislative powers retained, not the powers devolved. It should recognise that in certain fields legislative power needs to be shared between different levels of government, including Europe. That is easier to achieve with the continuing sovereignty of Parliament, which would enable Westminster to legislate even in transferred fields. Westminster's capacity to intervene should gradually become regulated by conventions; but the legislation should provide sufficient flexibility to enable either Government to legislate (by invitation or consent) on the territory of the other.

Chapter 6

Cabinet versus Local Government Model

Introduction

194 The previous two chapters have discussed the role and functions and the powers of the new Assembly. This chapter considers the Assembly's procedures and structure: how would it best be organised to perform the role and exercise the powers envisaged for it? Within the UK there are two models available: the **local government model,** whose committee structure merges the executive and scrutiny functions in a single body; and the **cabinet model,** which creates a separate executive body drawn from the Assembly and accountable to it.

195 A third (presidential) model carries the separation a stage further, by creating a directly elected separate executive body. This has occasionally been proposed in the UK: for example, in Michael Heseltine's and Tony Blair's expressions of interest in directly elected mayors[27], and in the Government's proposals in the Framework Documents for Northern Ireland for a directly elected executive body (the 'Panel').[28] It is not pursued further here, because none of the parties proposing a Welsh Assembly has suggested there should be separate elections for the Executive in Wales.

196 If the Assembly has legislative power then it is generally supposed that there should be a separate executive body, in order to maintain separation of powers. The converse does not necessarily follow, that an Assembly with executive power should adopt the local government model. A separate executive body is feasible in local government; and indeed is the norm in most other countries. The chapter therefore begins by discussing the respective merits of the local government and the cabinet model, and whether there is need for a separate executive body (referred to herafter as the Welsh Executive); and it concludes with a discussion of other lessons from elected assemblies in countries of a similar size to Wales.

The Local Government Model

197 The local government model was adopted in the Wales Act 1978, which conferred all powers upon the Assembly as a body corporate. The legislation specified that the Assembly should operate like local government, through multi-party subject committees, each of which would reflect the balance of representation in the Assembly (section 22). The Assembly was required to establish committees to cover the whole range of the devolved Government's subject responsibilities, and these committees could exercise powers and functions delegated by the Assembly (section 17). Each committee would have a chairman and a separate leader. The leader could exercise powers on behalf of the committee, and so represented a semi-executive within each committee: the legislation specified "the leader of a committee shall be known as its executive member" (section 17(2)(b)).

198 To give strategic and policy direction the Wales Act proposed an over-arching Executive Committee, composed of the leaders of all the other committees. Unlike the subject committees, this Committee could be single party, and the chairman of the Executive Committee would also be its leader. As such he or she would be the political leader of the Assembly. The Executive Committee would only be single party if one party had an overall majority in the Assembly, enabling it to control all the subject committees and to select their leaders. If no party had an overall majority the Executive Committee would be, in effect, a coalition, of the kind experienced in some hung local authorities in England.

199 The local government model generally has a fairly elaborate committee structure, because every function must be supervised by a committee or sub-committee of elected members. In **Table 6** is an illustrative model showing how the current functions of the Welsh Office could be brought under the control of local government style committees of the Assembly[29]. In addition to the main committees covering the nine different subject areas, there would need to be a finance committee, personnel committee, and legislation scrutiny committee; and there would need to be monitoring and liaison committees with local government, Westminster and the EU. Without some restructuring, the total number of committees (including sub-committees) might come to between 40 and 50. Each committee would be supported by the relevant group or division of the Welsh administration. The administration would be responsible to the Assembly as a whole, although on a day to day basis the officials would work to the committees and their leaders.

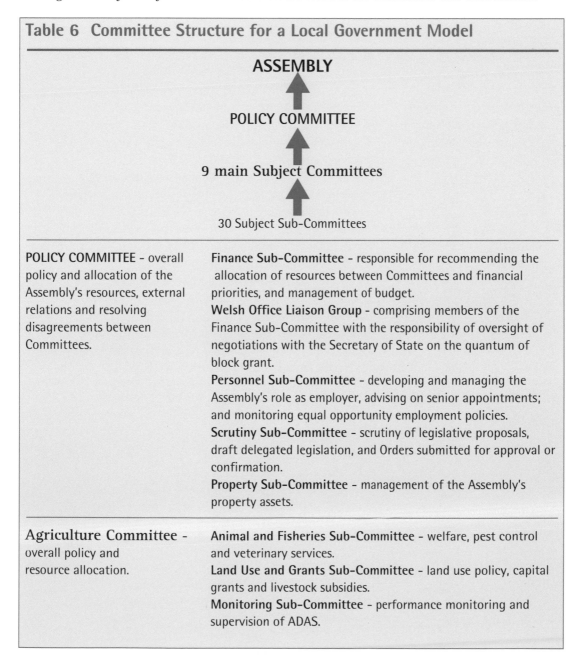

Table 6 Committee Structure for a Local Government Model

ASSEMBLY

↑

POLICY COMMITTEE

↑

9 main Subject Committees

↑

30 Subject Sub-Committees

POLICY COMMITTEE - overall policy and allocation of the Assembly's resources, external relations and resolving disagreements between Committees.	**Finance Sub-Committee** - responsible for recommending the allocation of resources between Committees and financial priorities, and management of budget. **Welsh Office Liaison Group** - comprising members of the Finance Sub-Committee with the responsibility of oversight of negotiations with the Secretary of State on the quantum of block grant. **Personnel Sub-Committee** - developing and managing the Assembly's role as employer, advising on senior appointments; and monitoring equal opportunity employment policies. **Scrutiny Sub-Committee** - scrutiny of legislative proposals, draft delegated legislation, and Orders submitted for approval or confirmation. **Property Sub-Committee** - management of the Assembly's property assets.
Agriculture Committee - overall policy and resource allocation.	**Animal and Fisheries Sub-Committee** - welfare, pest control and veterinary services. **Land Use and Grants Sub-Committee** - land use policy, capital grants and livestock subsidies. **Monitoring Sub-Committee** - performance monitoring and supervision of ADAS.

Education and Culture Committee - overall policy and resource allocation; including development of Welsh language policies.	**Schools Sub-Committee** - schools reorganisation, LMS, GMS, curriculum and monitoring of Curriculum Council. **Further and Higher Education Sub-Committee** - monitoring of establishments, Funding Councils, teacher training and supply, and tuition and student matters. **Community Sub-Committee** - policies on youth, community and adult education. Monitoring of capital grants to voluntary organisations. **Arts and Libraries Sub-Committee** - monitoring of the library service and arts grants, and supervision of Arts Council, National Library and National Museum. **Sports Sub-Committee** - sport and active recreation and supervision ofthe Sports Council. Grants to sports bodies. **Monitoring Sub-Committee** - performance monitoring and supervision of Schools Inspectorate.
Economic Development Committee - overall policy and resource allocation.	**Grants Sub-Committee** - administration of ERDF, RSA, UIG, SDS and other capital and revenue grants. **Monitoring Sub-Committee** - performance monitoring and supervision of DBRW, LAW, WDA and WTB. **Enterprise and Training Sub-Committee** - support for innovation, relevant project management, small business support, and monitoring and supervision of TECs.
Environmental Health Committee - overall policy and resource allocation.	**Waste Management Sub-Committee** - policy co-ordination and supervision of waste management. **Pollution and Coastal Protection Sub-Committee** - policy co-ordination, emergency planning, supervision and administration of funding. **Personal Services Sub-Committee** - policy co-ordination and supervision of trading standards, food and consumer protection, and Health Promotional Supervision of HPA.
Health Committee - overall policy and resource allocation.	**Hospital Services Sub-Committee** - estate management, building programme and supplies. Supervision of WHCSA and Health Authorities. **Medical Services Sub-Committee** - performance monitoring of NHS Trusts, and medical and ancillary staff. **Community Health Sub-Committee** - supervision of FHSAs, and policy development on general medical, dental, ophthalmic and pharmaceutical services including GPs.

Highways and Transportation Committee - overall policy and resource allocation.	**Strategic Network Sub-Committee** - policy and programming for strategic road schemes. **Trunk Roads Sub-Committee** - management of the trunk road programme and agency arrangements. **Highway Administration Sub-Committee** - consideration of applications from local authorities for road safety, and highway creation, diversion and extinguishment proposals. **Public Transport Sub-Committee** - development of policies for public transport.
Housing Committee - policy for public and private sector housing matters, including HSOP and Tenants' Charter responsibilities.	**Monitoring Sub-Committee** - including supervision of Housing for Wales.
Planning Committee - overall policy and resource allocation.	**Planning Policy Sub-Committee** - development policy and procedures, including planning guidance. **Planning Implementation Sub-Committee** - monitoring of implementation of national planning policy, and local plans; supervision of the Planning Inspectorate. **Conservation Sub-Committee** - development of Countryside and Conservation policies and supervision of CADW, Commission on Historical Monuments, Ancient Monuments Board and CCW.
Social Services Committee -overall policy and resource allocation.	**Child and Family Sub-Committee** - development of child and family services, child protection and abuse policies, adoption and maternity services. **Community Care Sub-Committee** - general policy for social and community care, including residential and nursing homes, terminal care and disability. **Monitoring Sub-Committee** - performance monitoring and supervision of Social Services Inspectorate.

200 There may be a difficulty, if too many committees are created, in obtaining sufficient expertise from amongst the members of the Assembly and sufficient commitment. Expertise can be drafted in through co-option (as happens in local government) and the use of special advisers (as happens at Westminster). Section 17 of the Wales Act 1978 limited membership of committees to Members of the Assembly, with no power to co-opt, and made no reference to the use of advisers.

201 The strengths of the local government model are that the formal decision-taking processes are open, and involve all the elected members. The committees meet in public, and under the Access to Information Act 1985 their papers and minutes are open to public inspection. Through sitting on committees backbenchers participate in executive decisions and the business of government, and do not feel so excluded and frustrated as do some backbenchers at Westminster.

202 But the local government model has also been the subject of recurring criticism. A series of official reports - Maud (1967), Bains (1972) and Widdicombe (1986) - have mounted a sustained critique of the committee system as a relic from the nineteenth century[30]. The system is cumbersome, with the potential for the same issue to be referred to several different committees; power is diffused, so that it is difficult to see where accountability lies; and there is a blurring of the executive and representative roles, to the disadvantage of both. Even the apparent openness and power sharing suggested by the multi-party committees is a bit of a smokescreen, since if a single party has a majority, the real decisions are often taken at party meetings held behind closed doors, and then forced through the committees, with little serious discussion, and no chance that they will be altered.

203 This critique is not confined to the Widdicombe report and the other official committees established by central government. The independent Commission for Local Democracy has said:

"[the local government model] is seriously inadequate to meet the requirements of a mature democracy. It obscures and distorts what should be open and lively political activity for the majority of citizens and it fails to supply clear lines of local accountability. The system encourages political parties to continue private informal management of councils and grants them inordinate power. The basis of local administration is both secretive in itself and confusing for the bulk of local people. From that confusion arises apathy and cynicism towards local democracy...we believe that revitalising local democracy demands that the Assembly and the Executive is separated".[31]

204 A similar critique was advanced by the Working Party on the Internal Management of Local Authorities in England (July 1993), a group with a strong majority of local government experts and representatives from the local authority associations. It said:

"the committee structure emerged and was developed at a time when local government was much less politicised than it is today...Most major policy decisions in practice are taken not by the full council, its committees or its sub-committees but elsewhere within the ruling group...The majority party, where there is one, through its lead members and especially its leader, is a de facto executive, given authority by the party group. Formal authority may rest with the full council, or with the committee, but the real authority rests with individuals and not with the committee or council structures...We believe that this inconsistency...is inherently unsatisfactory and prevents clear accountability.

Because the present legislative framework excludes the political group from a formal place in the decision-making process it prevents its development into a distinct body...Executive models provide clear political direction for the authority; make clear where accountability lies; provide a more efficient, quicker and co-ordinated decision making process..." [32]

The Cabinet Model

205 These proposals for a distinct executive body within local government come close to the cabinet model. The key difference in legislative terms is that with the cabinet model executive powers would be conferred not on the Assembly but on a separate Executive; as in central government where executive powers are conferred on Ministers rather than on Parliament or any of its committees. The Assembly would exercise powers of primary and secondary legislation, and

would call the Executive to account. Thus the cabinet model would separate executive functions on the one hand; and deliberative, legislative and scrutinising functions on the other. This separation is the norm in countries which follow the separation of powers: the Assembly needs to be a separate body in order to maintain an effective check upon the Executive.

206 This need not prevent the members of the Executive being drawn from the Assembly. The leader of the majority party would form an Executive, appoint the Executive Members, and distribute portfolios covering the devolved subject areas. An Executive of seven or eight members would seem sufficient to cover subjects now dealt with by three Government Ministers. How the Executive portfolios might be distributed is shown in **Table 7**. This is for illustrative purposes only: other permutations are possible.[33]

207 Each Executive Member would be supported by officials of the Welsh administration. The officials would be responsible to the Executive and not to the Assembly, although they could appear before Assembly committees to explain and answer questions on the Executive's policy and actions. The Assembly would need its own staff, separate from the Welsh administration, to act as its secretariat, service its committees, etc.

208 Most primary legislation would be proposed by the Executive, but backbench members could promote private members' bills. There would also have to be provision for private legislation in subject areas where the Assembly has legislative power (a good example would be the Cardiff Bay barrage scheme). Private bills could not be excluded; but their procedures would need to be greatly streamlined to make them manageable in a small Assembly. In addition to scrutinising the Executive, the Assembly could scrutinise the activities of Welsh quangos. The quangos would be appointed by and answerable to the Executive, but there could be a requirement that key appointments should be submitted to the Assembly for approval.

209 In addition to debating primary legislation, the Assembly would also have general debates on subjects of current interest, chosen by the Executive or the opposition parties. There could also be oral and written questions to Executive Members. The Assembly would undertake most of its scrutinising work through committees. There could be a requirement that each Executive Member should report to the relevant committee once a month or once a quarter on his/her area of responsibility.

210 The cabinet model has also come in for heavy criticism in recent years. The main charges against it are that it concentrates executive power in too few hands; it is excessively secret; backbenchers are excluded not merely from power but from any influence; the executive dominates the Assembly, and Ministerial accountability has become a threadbare convention.

Table 7: Welsh Executive Organisation Chart (Cabinet Model)

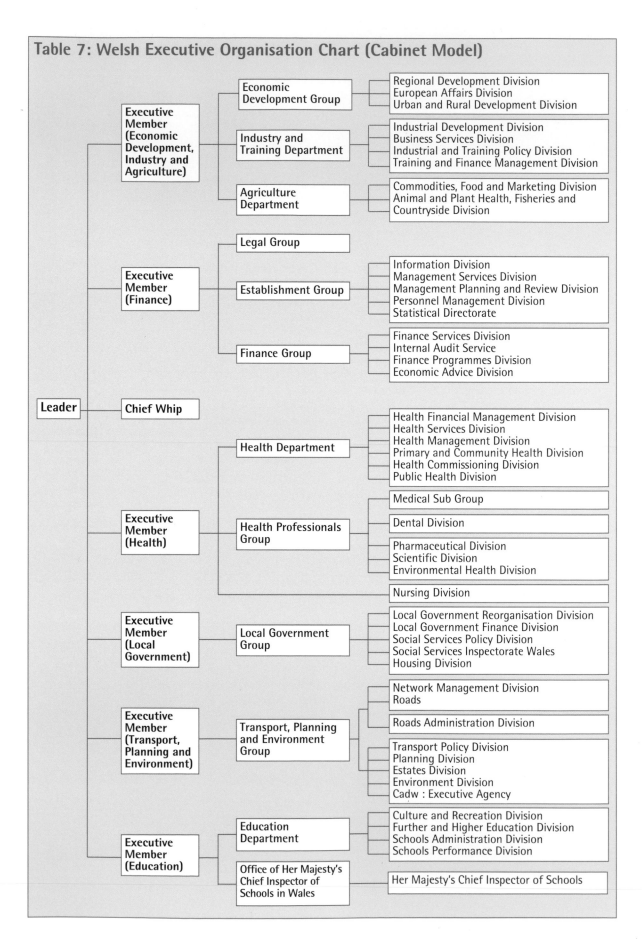

The Models Compared

211 It may be helpful at this point briefly to summarise the advantages and disadvantages of each model:

advantages of the local government model
- greater participation by all members through the subject committees.
- a capacity to work across party lines in multi-party committees.
- better access for the public to the decision taking process, as meetings of the Assembly and its committees would be open to the public.
- good understanding with local government, because both would operate under the same model.

disadvantages of the local government model
- drives real policy making into party meetings behind closed doors.
- difficult to develop corporate strategy.
- encourages parochialism in decision taking.
- Whitehall might find it less easy to co-operate.

advantages of the cabinet model
- small executive produces quicker and more effective decision taking.
- sharper accountability through separating executive action from the scrutiny and criticism of that action.
- executive can take a broad view, leaving backbenchers to promote constituency interests.

disadvantages of the cabinet model
- backbench members would have no role in decision taking.
- backbench activity may not be attractive to people of ability.
- government is more remote and less accessible for the public.

A Cabinet Model with Safeguards

212 We have set out the arguments at some length because this is an important decision for the design and working of the Welsh Assembly. We believe the balance of the argument comes down in favour of the cabinet model. The recurrent critique of the local government model cannot be ignored. Nor can the failure of local government over 30 years to respond to that critique. Local government is apparently more inclusive, through involving backbenchers and Opposition members on its executive committees; but this drives the real decision making underground into the party group. The Policy Committee in the local government model would become the *de facto* cabinet but without the open accountability mechanisms of cabinet government.

213 The signals conveyed by the model chosen are important in another respect. If executive power is conferred upon the Assembly and exercised through the traditional local government committee structure there is a risk of the Assembly being perceived as an over-grown county council. Scotland and Northern Ireland will both have parliamentary government, with separate Executives answerable to their respective parliaments; while Wales will have adopted a model which is distinctly second best.

214 Even if the Assembly has powers of secondary legislation only the critique of the local government model argues in favour of a separate Executive. But if the Assembly has primary legislative powers, like the proposed parliaments in Scotland and Northern Ireland, then separation of legislative power from executive power would be essential to reflect the basic constitutional doctrine of separation of powers (under which each branch of government is responsible for supplying checks and balances on the others): the need for such checks and balances is no less great in Wales than elsewhere.

215 But this does not mean that the Welsh Assembly should adopt the Westminster system lock, stock and barrel. There are weaknesses - severe weaknesses - in the relations between Westminster and Whitehall which a new Assembly should strive to avoid. Executive domination and excessive secrecy are not necessary features of the Westminster model, and a number of steps could be taken to build a different political culture in Wales:

- controlling the size of the payroll vote. Executive domination at Westminster is exacerbated by nearly one third of the members of the majority party being Ministers or otherwise on the Government payroll. There should be no need in the Assembly for junior Ministers; nor for PPSs or other kinds of political assistants. If (as is discussed in Chapter 11) the Assembly has 80-100 members, the maximum size of the Executive - including Whips - should be set at 10. That is 10-12.5% of the whole: in Australian state parliaments of comparable size (Queensland, South Australia, Western Australia) the average proportion is 13%. Another reason for controlling the size of the Executive in small Assemblies is to ensure that there are enough Government backbenchers to sit on the Assembly's committees.

- introduce freedom of information legislation. Local government is subject to the Access to Information Act 1985; there is no equivalent national legislation. If central government fails to introduce a Freedom of Information Act, one of the first actions of the Welsh Assembly could be to introduce a freedom of information regime for the Welsh Executive.

- make the Assembly master of its own procedure. Westminster relies upon a Government Minister (the Leader of the House) to propose changes to its procedures. The Assembly could assert early on its right to determine its own procedure.

- debate legislation in specialist committees. The select committees at Westminster do not scrutinise new legislation in their field; instead bills are referred to ad hoc standing committees with few if any experts on the subject matter of the bill.

216 This is not a full list, but a set of suggestions to illustrate the kinds of changes that might be made to break the Westminster mould. The need is underlined by the experience of the parliaments in the Australian states and Canadian provinces, many with populations similar to that of Wales. Most of the Canadian parliaments are between 50 (Newfoundland) and 130 members (Ontario) in size; and the Australian state parliaments range from 45 (Tasmania) to 177 (New South Wales). Politicisation and the power of the party caucus plus executive domination have combined to make many of the chambers pretty empty shells. The risk of executive domination seems to be greater in small parliaments because of the proportionately greater power of the executive in terms of direct patronage (the payroll vote) and indirect patronage through promises of appointments to quangos, etc.

217 There needs to be a strenuous effort from the start to avoid creating a scaled down version of Westminster. The scale is so different that the dynamics will be completely different. The Australian state parliaments sit for only 50 to 60 days a year; the largest Canadian ones (Ontario and Quebec) for only 100 days. Membership of most of these state legislatures is not a full-time

occupation; and the same is likely to hold true in Wales. Nor do they have the size to support an elaborate committee structure: most of the Canadian parliaments have between six and nine committees, and the smaller ones tend to debate legislation in a committee of the whole house. The first Leader and Leader of the Opposition, plus the Speaker and Principal Clerk of the Welsh Assembly would do well to visit some of these commonwealth parliaments. It will not be easy to find time early in the life of the new Assembly; but the standing orders should be informed by a range of experience wider than Westminster.

218 There is a comprehensive analysis and thought provoking set of proposals in Bernard Crick and David Millar's draft Standing Orders for the Scottish Parliament[34]. The authors issue the cautionary reminder that in the 1920s both Stormont and the Dail in Dublin carried on with Westminster practices to an extraordinary degree. This was no considered tribute, certainly not in the case of Dublin, but simply reflected lack of forethought and pressure of other business. If the Welsh Assembly wants to break from the Westminster mould it will need to make conscious efforts to do so.

Conclusion

219 The legislation needs to confer executive power on the Assembly (the local government model) or upon a separate Executive (the cabinet model). The local government model has been criticised for its cumbersome committee structure, slow decision taking, diffusion of responsibility, and relegation of real policy making to the party caucus. The cabinet model is criticised for its concentration of power, excessive secrecy, executive domination, and exclusion of backbenchers. The chapter concludes in favour of the cabinet model, but with safeguards to avoid the worst features of Westminster and to give backbenchers a proper and satisfying role.

Chapter 7

Relations between the Assembly and Central Government

Introduction

220 The next three chapters of the report consider the Assembly's relations with other levels of government: with Westminster, quangos, local government and the European Union. Of these the most important is Westminster. The UK Government will continue to determine the annual block grant to Wales; it will be responsible for a range of reserved powers such as social security which will have a major impact in Wales; and it will be responsible for the negotiation and implementation of EC laws. In all these fields it is vital to put in place structures which promote a co-operative and not an antagonistic relationship.

The Secretary of State for Wales

221 The most obvious link between the institutions of Welsh and UK Government is the Secretary of State for Wales. Under the Wales Act 1978 the post was retained and the Secretary of State was given significant oversight powers in relation to the devolution settlement. The report of the Royal Commission on the Constitution had suggested that the post be dropped, but the government rejected that proposal while acknowledging (in relation to both the Scottish and Welsh Secretaries) that "major changes and a diminution in their present powers would be an inevitable consequence of a substantial measure of devolution; careful thought will have to be given to their precise role".[35]

Possible Functions

222 The role of the Secretary of State post-devolution can be analysed into five possible functions[36]:
- **midwife functions:** managing the elections for the Assembly, arranging the first meeting, transferring Welsh Office staff and assets to the new Welsh Executive.
- **continuity functions:** inviting someone to form a Government; formal appointments to the executive; appointing a caretaker Government if the Government loses its majority.
- **veto functions.**
- **as the channel of communications with the EC.**
- **as a UK Cabinet Minister, and chief adviser to the UK Government on Welsh affairs.**

These are examined below.

Midwife Functions

223 In implementing the devolution legislation and setting up the Assembly the Secretary of State will have a vital role. That role could extend into the early months and even years of devolution as the UK and devolved Governments begin to establish working relations. Both sides will be feeling their way, and there may be much to be said for retaining a Secretary of State in the Cabinet to take the lead in an important and sensitive process.

224 After these early months the role of the Secretary of State becomes much more questionable. Neither the Secretary of State nor his small department will have the expertise to continue to negotiate with the devolved Government over its expenditure and block grant. Such negotiations in reality will be conducted between the Welsh Executive and the Treasury. If the Secretary of State acts as a channel for those negotiations, both the Minister and the department will quickly be reduced to acting as a post office.

225 The same is true for discussions between the Westminster and devolved Governments over legislation and other issues in the devolved subject areas. The Welsh Executive is bound to deal directly with the Department of the Environment over e.g. housing, environmental protection and land use planning; and with the Department of Health on disease prevention, community care and cross-border patient flows. The Secretary of State's department will have no knowledge or expertise in these matters and, if involved at all, could again act only as a post office. As to the Secretary of State's 'governor general' functions, the main ones are overseeing Assembly elections, and inviting an Assembly member to form an Executive. These seem hardly sufficient to justify retaining a Cabinet Minister specifically for the purpose; but they do briefly deserve separate mention.

Continuity Functions

226 Supervising the elections to the Assembly will be the main continuity function. The Wales Act 1978 specified a fixed term Assembly, with elections on the third Thursday in March every four years. But in section 2(2) it gave the Secretary of State the discretion to vary this date by up to two months either way. The House of Lords insisted that what the Government described as "a matter of simple administrative convenience" should be subject to parliamentary approval. Their fear was that this limited power to determine the election date could be used to gain political advantage. The scope for political manipulation that this section introduced probably out-weighs the advantage of the flexibility it provided. If the Assembly is to be elected for a fixed term, then it should remain fixed.

227 A related point is the timing of elections following a dissolution. The Scotland Act 1978 allowed dissolution if two thirds of the membership voted for it. The setting of these dates then fell to the Secretary of State, again within strict constraints. Yet in the case of by-elections the presiding officer or Speaker of the Assembly took this role. There seems no reason why he or she should not perform the same function following dissolution, provided that the election has to take place within, say, two months of the resolution to dissolve.

228 The other continuity function relates to the selection, appointment and dismissal of the Welsh Executive. Here too we need to look at the Scotland Act 1978, because the Wales Act did not provide for a separate Executive. The Act placed the onus on the Assembly to elect the First Secretary, which person would then be automatically appointed by the Secretary of State. In the event of the Assembly failing to agree on a candidate, the Secretary of State had power to appoint. In their draft Standing Orders for a Scottish Parliament, Bernard Crick and David Millar suggest instead an exhaustive ballot to try to ensure that the choice remains with the elected body.[37]

229 This is not an entirely hypothetical question, as events in Australia have shown[38]. Crick and Millar are right to ensure that the system of selection remains with the elected body; it is an essentially political process which should be left to the local politicians. The method of appointment should then be a formality. If the Welsh Executive is a Crown body the appointment should be by the Crown or a representative of the Crown. But there should be no place for prerogative power which leaves any room for discretion or ambiguity; the appointment should be strictly a formality.

Veto Functions

230 The Wales Act 1978 contained veto powers for the Secretary of State to direct the Assembly to take or not to take action (section 34) or to revoke delegated legislation made by the Assembly (section 35) if it might affect a reserved matter, or was incompatible with Community or international obligations. Apart from the need to enforce the UK's international obligations such a wide override power seems unacceptable today. The formal means for the resolution of disputes should ultimately be through the courts, but only after political negotiations have been exhausted; and with the implicit reserve power for Westminster to legislate in any area as the last resort.

Adviser to UK Government on Welsh Affairs

231 As we have indicated above, responsibility for defending and promoting Welsh interests will fall after devolution to the Welsh Assembly and Executive, and not the Secretary of State with a seat in the UK Cabinet. But the UK Government will need a source of political advice on how to manage the relationship with Wales. Other Ministers might need guidance on the limits of their responsibilities with respect to Wales following devolution. There will have to be a channel for the flow of information in both directions between Cardiff and London. All of these roles would fall naturally to the Secretary of State for Wales initially, but in the longer term might suit a Secretary of State for Territorial Affairs responsible for devolution to Scotland and Northern Ireland as well.

Managing the Transition and Beyond

232 The role of manager of relations with Wales and keeper of the devolution settlement may be a real one, but it does not represent a separate Cabinet post. The other functions identified above are either undesirable in principle (veto), temporary (midwife) or easily distributed elsewhere. But the first role is important and may well expand over time. This suggests a two-stage approach to the Secretary of State for Wales' future role:

- the Secretary of State remains in place to perform the midwife functions in establishing a Welsh Assembly and to continue to be responsible for residual powers left to 'the Secretary of State' under the devolution legislation; but

- during the remainder of the Westminster parliamentary term a key part of the role, in conjunction with the Secretary of State for Scotland (who will be similarly placed) should be to devise coherent proposals in the light of experience for the future of both posts.

233 This could lead to the establishment over time of a Minister in the Cabinet with responsibility for intergovernmental relations with the territories of the UK. The pace of that development is difficult to judge: the role may include Scotland and Wales from day one, and it may include Northern Ireland before the end of the Parliament. Or it may be a role that is recognised from the start of the legislative programme for constitutional reform, namely a Cabinet Minister with constitutional matters as a sole responsibility. In that event the Secretaries of State for Scotland and Wales could be absorbed into the wider role.

Representation at Westminster: the West Lothian Question

234 During the devolution debates in the 1970s the 'West Lothian Question' was described by Francis Pym as "the single most contentious problem to arise in our debates on the [Scotland and Wales] Bill..."[39]. It was named after Tam Dalyell, Labour MP for West Lothian, who persistently challenged the Government about the continuing role of Scottish MPs at Westminster once Scotland had its own Assembly north of the border. Where was the justice in allowing Scottish MPs to vote on English business when English MPs could not speak and vote on Scottish matters devolved to the new Assembly? The question was raised less sharply in relation to Wales, perhaps because the Welsh Assembly would not have had powers of primary legislation, and Wales had half the number of Scottish MPs. If the Welsh Assembly has powers of primary legislation, then the question will arise equally sharply in the case of Wales: there will be a 'West Glamorgan' question about the role of the Welsh MPs remaining at Westminster.

235 In fact, the question will arise even if the Assembly has powers of secondary legislation only, in relation to Welsh MPs voting on English secondary legislation, and asking questions about English matters which are devolved subjects in Wales. The question is all the sharper because Wales is already over-represented at Westminster. It has 38 MPs (40 after the boundary changes which take effect at the next election), when in population terms its quota should be 33. Scotland is also over-represented (72 seats when a *pro rata* allocation would give Scotland 59). It is commonly supposed that this over-representation is deliberate policy, to avoid over large geographical constituencies in sparsely populated rural areas. In fact the over-representation has arisen by historical accident: in Scotland's case following the withdrawal of the 100 Irish MPs in 1922, which adjusted all the territorial ratios at Westminster; and in Wales' case following the Speaker's Conference of 1944 which institutionalised the over-representation of Scotland and Wales within the modern boundary review system. The most recent historical survey concludes that "the over-representation of Scotland and Wales arises not from considerations of principle, but from the bargained compromises of 1944, which have been frozen into the legislation governing the allocation of seats"[40].

236 The West Lothian Question is often regarded as insoluble; and it tends to be put by anti-devolutionists as an argument which undermines the whole devolution policy rather than a difficulty to be resolved. Before considering the possible solutions, it is worth turning the question round and posing the converse Westminster question: where is the justice in allowing English MPs to speak and vote on business of exclusive interest to Wales? This is not purely a hypothetical question, because as we have shown in this report, English MPs have been brought onto the Welsh standing committee to provide the Government with a majority to get its Welsh legislation through: and English MPs have tabled large numbers of oral Questions to Welsh Office Ministers, reducing the opportunities for Welsh MPs.

237 This point simply underlines that the existing system is not free of anomalies in its operation. Ferdinand Mount has written about the existing anomalies, and argues that it is the belief that there has to be symmetry in any arrangements for territorial government which makes the West Lothian question difficult for devolutionists to answer. The UK has had and continues to have many examples of asymmetry, the Northern Ireland Parliament being the most obvious recent instance; and any political system will have 'anomalies' - such as the Scottish and Welsh over-representation at Westminster - which may have to be accepted:

"as for the 'West Lothian question', it is answered by existing practice. MPs are constantly voting on Bills which do not apply to them or their constituents. Membership of any political community entails acceptance of its anomalies...Anomalies follow from the uneven, asymmetrical nature of all existing societies and so must be endured;...[To] understand that political arrangements at any given moment can never be perfectly harmonious and symmetrical in every respect is the condition of a durable polity."[41]

'Solutions' to the West Lothian Question

238 As for 'solutions' to the West Lothian Question, the full range was considered in relation to the Irish Question which dominated parliamentary debate in the era from Gladstone to Lloyd George; and the three solutions on offer today were tried in the three Home Rule Bills of 1886, 1893 and 1912. The first, in 1886, was to remove Irish representation at Westminster completely. It was a logical answer, and understandable given Parliament's frustration at the obstructive tactics of the Irish MPs; but it would have replaced one injustice with a greater one, and subjected the Irish to taxation without representation. It is unthinkable, in today's terms, that so long as Westminster decides on defence, foreign affairs, taxation and social security for Wales, that Wales should not continue to be represented at Westminster.

239 The second solution, the 'in and out' rule was tried in the Government of Ireland Bill of 1893. This proposed a slight reduction in the number of Irish MPs (from 105 to 80), but would have prevented them voting on non-Irish business. This also is a logical answer, but would have given rise to immense difficulties in practice; and Gladstone withdrew the proposal during the committee stage of the Bill. The Government's majority would have changed from day to day, depending on the nature of the business being discussed; and as Tam Dalyell has pointed out, it would have been highly contentious deciding in any particular debate whether the Scottish and Welsh MPs were 'in' or 'out':

"one cannot have Members of the same Parliament with different functions and different limitations...Rules would have to be drawn up whereby one could decide on which issues the Scots and the Welsh could and could not vote: yet...it would be almost impossible for the Chair to pronounce satisfactorily on this...the Speaker would be put in a highly invidious position - and he would inevitably be drawn into the hurly-burly of party politics."[42]

240 The third solution is a reduction in the number of Welsh and Scottish MPs. This was the solution adopted in the Government of Ireland Act 1914, which proposed a total of 42 Irish MPs at Westminster, but no 'in and out' restrictions on their activities. The Act was not brought into operation because of the First World War; but in the Government of Ireland Act 1920, which did finally bring Home Rule to part of Ireland, a similar reduction was followed. Northern Ireland was given 13 MPs (including one university seat) in recognition of devolution to Stormont, where the six counties of Ulster had previously returned 28 MPs to Westminster.

241 Reduced representation is not strictly an 'answer' to the West Lothian Question, because if it is wrong for 40 Welsh MPs to vote on English business for which they have no responsibility it is no less wrong for 20 MPs to do so. But it is an understandable political response: and the Irish debates are instructive in demonstrating how Gladstone and Lloyd George, having explored the more 'logical' solutions concluded in favour of the political response. Such a political response may be called for in the case of Scotland and Wales, particularly in view of their current over-

representation. As we have shown, the over-representation is the product of historical accident, not deliberate policy; and it may prove difficult to ask English MPs to swallow that Scotland and Wales should have their devolved Assemblies **and** maintain their over-representation at Westminster. The Royal Commission on the Constitution came down in favour of reducing representation at Westminster to answer the West Lothian Question; and the precedent of Stormont also points to reduced representation.

242 All practical responses may thus come down to how far representation at Westminster should be reduced; and how that question should be decided. The accepted mechanism for changing the number of parliamentary seats in the past has been a Speaker's Conference. The last such Conference was convened in 1978 to consider Northern Ireland representation at Westminster following the abolition of Stormont in 1973 (and recommended an increase in the number of Northern Irish MPs from 12 to 17). The Government could propose such a conference before introducing devolution legislation, to indicate its willingness to review the question of Scottish and Welsh representation; but the Conference need not be convened until later in the Parliament, when there is some experience of the operation of the new Assemblies, and a better sense of the likelihood of any wider reforms (such as devolution to England). The 73 Scottish and 40 Welsh MPs returned at the next election could not be unseated for the duration of the Parliament, so there may be no need for an instant response; but there may need to be some response for the devolution legislation to be accepted as a fair settlement so far as the English are concerned.

243 The use of Speaker's Conferences was examined in the Constitution Unit's earlier report *Delivering Constitutional Reform*, which concluded:

> "*the future use of a Speaker's Conference depends upon whether it is judged appropriate for a particular issue to be considered in this way. For example, the use of a Speaker's Conference to decide on levels of Scottish representation in Westminster was raised by the Opposition during attempts at devolution in the 1970s. The Labour government resisted this suggestion on the grounds that the involvement of the Speaker in such a potentially controversial debate would considerably weaken the position of the Speaker. As explored by David Butler in Modifying Electoral Arrangements, there is evidence of reluctance on the part of previous Speakers to become involved in controversial electoral issues: '..although Speaker's Conferences seemed to have become established as part of the Constitution, their record is not very impressive either on achieving consensus on controversial matters or in seeing their recommendations translated into law.' "*[43]

244 Alternatives to a Speaker's Conference would be a select committee, which would provide a more open forum for the discussion of constitutional changes (and has a precedent on the Home Affairs Committee's report on the redistribution of Commons seats in 1987); or an Electoral Commission, which both the Labour Party and the Liberal Democrats have pledged to establish. The possibility of a change in the electoral system for the House of Commons (again, in prospect under a Labour or Liberal Democrat Government) also affords a reason for postponing any review of Welsh representation at Westminster, and might provide the context for a wider solution. If the outcome of the referendum is a change in the electoral system, Welsh representation could be revised as part of the wider change. If the outcome of the referendum is no change, the process might still leave machinery which could then be used to review Scottish and Welsh representation. These possibilities will be explored further in Unit reports to be published later in the year.

245 If the number of Welsh MPs is reduced that would alter the 40 Westminster constituencies which are likely to form the basis of the electoral system for the Welsh Assembly (discussed in Chapter 11). That need not hold up the first elections to the Assembly, nor need it necessarily require a revision of Assembly constituencies thereafter: these could continue to be based on the old Westminster constituencies even if Westminster moves on.

Welsh or UK Civil Service

246 When Northern Ireland gained its own Parliament it also established a separate Northern Ireland Civil Service. The report of the Royal Commission on the Constitution concluded that the same arrangement should apply for Scotland and Wales: the devolved administrations would want to choose their own senior officials, might not be content for general personnel matters to be handled by Whitehall, and would want to be able to rely on the undivided loyalty of their officials dealing with the Government, for example when negotiating the block grant.

247 The Government had reservations about this conclusion and did not provide for a separate civil service in the Wales Act 1978. They noted that a separate service would be more costly, because it would have to duplicate many of the central administrative functions in Cardiff; and they saw advantage in maintaining a unified civil service in allowing the Welsh administration to draw its officials from a wider pool of talent, and in fostering the co-operative relationships with other departments which were required to make devolution work.

248 Where does the balance of argument lie today? If anything, developments in the civil service since the 1970s have brought the two positions closer together. The Government's recent White Paper about the civil service[44] proposed a number of changes designed to devolve greater autonomy to individual departments to manage their staff and resources, whilst "the defining principles and standards of the civil service will continue to be centrally prescribed and mandatory for all departments and agencies".

249 These changes have created a potentially more encouraging framework in which to realise the benefits of maintaining a unified civil service. The experience of working closely with officials in other member states of the EU has exposed much of Whitehall to forms of intergovernmental co-operation in a way which was not true in the 1970s. A greater delegation of authority for pay, staff structures, management, etc. from April 1996 will also give a Welsh administration flexibility within a unified service. And more open recruitment practices for the senior civil service, including from outside government, will emphasise the benefits of the 'wide pool of talent' identified in the 1970s (the post of Permanent Secretary in the Welsh Office, for example, was advertised for the first time in March 1996, following Michael Scholar's transfer to the DTI).

250 Some of these arguments cut both ways: with a greater fragmentation of the civil service into Next Steps executive agencies, and planned privatisation of the Recruitment and Assessment Service, there is less and less of a unified civil service to belong to; and the fragmentation may impair mobility. For now the balance of advantage might lie with maintaining the link with the Home Civil Service, but encouraging the Welsh administration to consider establishing a separate Welsh Civil Service in the future: or a Welsh Public Service, to interchange with officials working in local government, the health service and in quangos. Whichever model is

chosen the important features to retain and build in are open competition (whether through the Civil Service Commission or otherwise); and inter-change with local government, Whitehall, and the European Union. Some 20 to 30 officials are on secondment from the Welsh Office at any one time (including to organisations outside the civil service). They must continue to have the opportunity to work in other central departments (the Treasury, Cabinet Office, UKRep in Brussels; and to participate in the UK's European Fast Stream programme which seeks to prepare UK candidates to win posts in EU institutions); and also to exchange more than the Welsh Office has done hitherto with local government. This will help them gain invaluable experience of how the system operates; and should help to dispel notions of 'us and them' between Cardiff and London, and between Cardiff and Welsh local authorities.

Interlocking Machinery

251 The overwhelming majority of Welsh Office officials will transfer to the staff of the new Welsh administration. The Secretary of State will initially need a small department, which will presumably continue to be known as the Welsh Office; but it can be very small, since the Secretary of State will have no direct responsibilities in the devolved subjects. It will probably comprise a private office and press office in Whitehall, and a small group of officials based in Cardiff to advise on relations with the devolved administration, and to support the Secretary of State in his or her role as Cabinet Minister and adviser to the UK Government on Welsh affairs.

252 Relations between Cardiff, Westminster and Whitehall will continue to be very close. Whatever the formal division of competences, there will be overlap between Welsh and UK interests across the board. Policies pursued in London will have an impact in Wales and vice versa. Two areas of particular mutual concern are Europe and finance (covered in chapters 9 and 10). But the need for co-operation, and possibly for institutional machinery to bolster it, goes far wider. The German system with its interlocking committees between the federal and Länder governments, and between the Länder themselves, illustrates how 'co-operative federalism' needs strong political and administrative machinery to underpin it and make it work in practice.

253 The machinery associated with devolution to Wales need not be as comprehensive as that for federal states like Germany, but it too will need intergovernmental arrangements. These might include:
- the intergovernmental machinery discussed in chapter 9 for co-ordination of European policy and chapter 10 for financial and economic policy.
- the presence of members of the Welsh Assembly in a reformed House of Lords by analogy with the Bundesrat, discussed in chapter 12.
- maintenance of the existing range of contacts between Welsh officials and their opposite numbers in Whitehall.
- the establishment of a new range of contacts with other devolved administrations: initially Scotland and Northern Ireland, and perhaps in due course the English regions.

254 Two positive things can be done to make sure these intergovernmental arrangements work smoothly:
- the Secretary of State for Wales should see it as an important part of his or her role to facilitate the development of these co-operative relationships. It may require an initial push to establish a pattern of co-operation and sharing of information.

- in addition to the Secretary of State initially retaining a small liaison office in Cardiff, the Welsh administration will also require a London office. This may sound like unnecessary overlap but the success of these two offices in establishing close links between Cardiff, Whitehall and Westminster in the early years of devolution could have a significant impact on the success or failure of the venture.

Conclusion

255 The Secretary of State will have a vital role in establishing the Assembly and in ensuring a smooth transition of functions from the Welsh Office to the devolved administration. Thereafter the main spokesman for Welsh interests will be the leader of the Welsh Assembly. For the UK Government there will continue to be an important role in managing relations with Wales, but this does not justify a separate Cabinet post. The task of upholding the devolution settlement is likely to fall to a Cabinet Minister with general responsibility for intergovernmental relations with the nations of the UK - Scotland, Wales and Northern Ireland.

256 The West Lothian Question is likely to arise just as sharply in any devolution debate in the 1990s as it did in the 1970s. The Government cannot ignore it, particularly since Wales is already over-represented at Westminster. One response would be to offer a review of Scottish and Welsh representation once the devolved Assemblies are established; another would be to consider the matter as part of wider changes to the electoral system for the House of Commons.

257 The new Welsh administration should initially be part of the Home Civil Service, but could later establish a separate Welsh Civil Service. Whichever model is chosen it is important to retain open competition; the civil service code of conduct; and a strong programme of inter-change between local government, Whitehall and Europe. Formal machinery is also necessary to underpin these informal exchanges and contacts, and to establish from the start a pattern of co-operation and sharing of information.

Chapter 8

Quangos in Wales

Introduction

258   In recent years there has been mounting public concern in Wales about the proliferation of quangos, people appointed to their boards, their operating expenses and lack of public accountability. Concern has been triggered by a few high-profile executive bodies with paid board members, big budgets and significant impact on the Welsh economy; but in public debate it has turned into a wider concern, and questioning about the need for quangos generally.

259   To date, this debate has taken place with little awareness of the great range and variety of quangos and their different functions. This chapter therefore begins by drawing a map of the Welsh quango state before considering the implications for quangos of a Welsh Assembly. The questions explored are whether these bodies should continue their arms-length relationship with Government in Wales; whether their functions should be absorbed by Government or the Assembly; and whether any quangos might be absorbed by local government or move towards increased local authority control.

A Map of the Welsh Quango State

260   There is no agreed definition of a quango, which makes it difficult to judge statements about the extent to which the 'quango state' has shrunk or grown. **Appendix A** lists the Non-Departmental Public Bodies (NDPBs) in Wales given in the official publication, *Public Bodies,* which defines a Non-Departmental Public Body as "a body which has a role in the processes of national government, but is not a government department or part of one, and accordingly operates to a greater or lesser extent at arm's length from Ministers". It goes on to divide quangos into three broad categories: executive bodies, advisory bodies and tribunals. However, reecent academic commentators have criticised the narrow scope of the Government's definition of NDPBs[45]. The scope of this chapter therefore embraces all the NDPBs listed in *Public Bodies;* NHS bodies (also recorded in *Public Bodies*); and Training and Enterprise Councils (which are not). The reason for including the TECs is that they are recipients of significant Government funding, they operate under tight Government contracts, and they were created to deliver Government training programmes.

261   It is difficult to convey the extraordinary range and variety of public bodies and quangos operating in Wales. For that the reader must turn to the list of the 176 public bodies recorded in **Appendix B** to which the Secretary of State for Wales made appointments as of September 1995[46]. About one-quarter of these bodies are England and Wales, GB or UK bodies to which the Welsh Secretary makes joint appointments or recommends suitable Welsh appointees to the main sponsoring department. What is striking about the list is the low profile of the majority of bodies recorded there. They are mainly specialised, technical bodies operating in relatively narrow fields where the Government needs independent advice, with the members giving their time free and receiving only expenses.

262   It is also important to note that, although the term is relatively new, quangos are not a new phenomenon. The earliest of the public bodies listed in **Appendix A**, the National Library of Wales and the National Museum of Wales, were established by Royal Charters issued in 1907. Nor are quangos a Conservative phenomenon. Of the executive bodies listed in **Appendix A**,

one third were created by Labour Governments: a proportion roughly equal to Labour's share of periods in office since the Second World War. It has suited Governments of both persuasions to create semi-independent bodies to carry out public functions for a variety of reasons: to bring in specialist expertise, to confer greater operational freedom, to remove the function from local authority or party political control, or simply to deliver programmes in a different way.

The Different Types of Quango

Executive Bodies

263 Executive bodies carry out a range of executive functions that would otherwise be carried out by a mainstream part of elected government at either central or local level. A number distribute Government funding (Arts Council, Sports Council, Higher and Further Education Funding Councils, Tai Cymru); others promote economic development (Welsh Development Agency, Land Authority for Wales, Development Board for Rural Wales, Cardiff Bay Development Corporation); yet others set standards and act as regulatory bodies (Curriculum and Assessment Authority for Wales, Welsh National Board for Nursing, Midwifery and Health Visiting). They generally employ their own staff and control their own budgets. There are nineteen executive bodies listed in **Appendix** A operating under the control of the Welsh Office.

Advisory Bodies

264 Advisory bodies are largely bodies set up by Ministers to provide specialist advice which is not available within the department. Examples in Wales include the Agricultural Advisory Panel, the Ancient Monuments Board, Historic Buildings Council, Local Government Boundary Commission, the Welsh Economic Council, Welsh Industrial Development Advisory Board and Welsh Scheme for the Development of Health and Social Research. They do not normally employ their own staff or have a separate budget. There are 24 advisory bodies operating in Wales, the great majority of whose members give their time free.

Tribunals

265 Tribunals are bodies with jurisdiction in a specialised field of law. They are generally serviced by staff from the sponsoring department. In Wales there are four exclusively Welsh tribunals - the Agricultural Land Tribunal, the Mental Health Review Tribunal for Wales, the Rent Assessment Panel, and the Valuation Tribunals (Wales). There are also many other tribunals with national jurisdiction, such as the Lands Tribunal.

NHS Bodies

266 Although NHS bodies are not normally classified as NDPBs, there seems no reason why they should be regarded or treated as different from them. They are responsible for significant amounts of public expenditure; some £2bn in 1993-94. Health also accounts for a large number of specialist advisory bodies: one-third of the 24 advisory bodies in Wales operate in the fields of health and medical education.

Training and Enterprise Councils

267 TECs are established as non-profit making private sector companies, limited by guarantee, with boards composed of local business people. They provide training programmes for unemployed and unskilled workers of the kind formerly delivered by the Manpower Services Commission and the Training Agency. Although not normally considered to be NDPBs, TECs have their budget

and corporate plans approved by the Welsh Office. They work under contract to the Welsh Office with tight monitoring of their targets and performance standards. The total budgets of the seven Welsh TECs came to £100m in 1994-95.

Public Concern about Quangos

268 Despite the generalised nature of public concern, it has really focused on a few high profile executive bodies with paid board members, big budgets and significant impact on the Welsh economy. It is not the Agricultural Wages Committees, the Royal Commission on Ancient and Historical Monuments for Wales, nor the Library and Information Services Council which hit the headlines: they form part of the hidden 90% of quangos which quietly get on with their jobs, may deserve to be better known, but would probably not cause significant public concern if they were.

269 Concern centres on quangos with executive functions. Apart from the NHS bodies and TECs there are only eleven Welsh NDPBs with annual budgets of more than £10m. Of these just a few high profile bodies have aroused public concern: the Welsh Development Agency and Development Board for Rural Wales following financial scandals; and the Cardiff Bay Development Corporation, Land Authority for Wales and Tai Cymru have encountered criticism for their lack of democratic legitimacy.

Nature of Public Criticism

270 The main criticisms levelled at these bodies are their inadequate accountability; removal of functions from local government; the nature of the people appointed to their boards; lapses in their internal management. Health Promotion Wales has also caused concern in relation to travel expenses of the former Chief Executive, and the Arts Council of Wales for certain of its funding decisions (it was subsequently cleared by the National Audit Office). More generally there is a wider concern at the secretiveness with which certain quangos operate, particularly when contrasted with the openness regime which applies by law to local authorities.

Inadequate Accountability

271 There is no direct local accountability for these bodies. Formally the line of accountability lies through Ministers to Parliament. There is also financial accountability of each Chief Executive (as the appointed Accounting Officer) to the Public Accounts Committee. The Public Accounts Committee can and does summon the Accounting Officers to appear before it. The last Chief Executive of the Welsh Development Agency resigned after a Public Accounts Committee appearance.

Removal of Functions from Local Government

272 It is often asserted that the growth of quangos has been at the expense of local government. This is only partially true: the vast majority of the quangos listed in **Appendices A and B** operate in areas which were never local government responsibilities. But Tai Cymru - Housing for Wales has assumed most of the responsibilities for funding the building of social housing which lay with the Welsh District Councils; and the County Councils lost control of further education to the Further Education Funding Council for Wales. Local authorities have also lost their rights to nominate Councillors to form the majority of the membership of police authorities, and their right to nominate any members at all to the health authorities.

Board Appointments

273 The media and opposition parties have frequently claimed that Welsh quangos contain disproportionate numbers of businessmen, lawyers and accountants, and politicians or sympathisers who having failed to get elected have been appointed to public positions instead. A number of quangos seem to be run by a small circle of establishment figures who hold multiple appointments. It is also said that some appointments have been made with inadequate enquiries about the individual's suitability for the post.

274 This is one area where the Government has started to act, following the stringent criticisms made by the Committee on Standards in Public Life (the Nolan Committee). Chapter 4 of the Nolan Committee's first report (May 1995)[47] concerned quangos, and recommended sweeping changes to the appointments process and the rules on propriety. Nolan even considered removing powers of patronage from Ministers to an independent body, but concluded that responsibility should remain with Ministers, but subject to stringent safeguards.

275 The Nolan Committee's principal recommendations to tighten up the appointments process were as follows:
- appointments on the basis of merit, to form boards with a balance of relevant skills and backgrounds.
- published job descriptions to define the task and the qualities sought.
- transparency about the appointments process.
- identifying a wide range of candidates through:
  - advertising
  - executive search
  - consultation with interested bodies, user groups and local authorities.
- independent advisory panel to vet all candidates.
- reappointments only after a review of the postholder's performance.
- a Public Appointments Commissioner should be appointed to regulate, monitor, and report on the public appointments process.

276 Sir Leonard Peach took up office in December 1995 as the Public Appointments Commissioner, and all appointments by the Welsh Office will now be subject to his scrutiny. The Welsh Office will have to establish an independent advisory panel or committee, and report annually on the public appointments made by the department. If in future these appointments are made by the devolved Government in Wales, they could initially continue to be subject to scrutiny by the Public Appointments Commissioner. In time Wales will probably want to appoint its own guardian; but he or she will need to work closely alongside the Public Appointments Commissioner to ensure that Wales conforms to best practice throughout the UK.

Independent Quangos after Devolution

277 It is sometimes suggested that a Welsh Assembly will provide a complete solution to the quango problem: appointed boards can be abolished and all functions transferred to appropriate committees of the Assembly. That will not be possible if (as discussed in Chapter 6) the committees have not executive but scrutinising functions. But in any event the range, variety and sheer numbers of the quangos recorded in **Appendices A and B** must give pause to anyone advocating wholesale abolition. Restructuring will certainly be required; but those contemplating abolition need to be aware of the reasons why functions are given to quangos in the first place. These may still offer

sound reasons for leaving the functions with an independent body, but with a more open system of appointment, and operating within a tighter framework of democratic accountability.

278   Abolitionists also need to be realistic about the cost savings which might flow from abolition. The quangos' administration costs could not simply be absorbed by the Welsh Assembly or local authorities, but would need to be transferred along with the functions. The total staff employed by the 19 quangos listed in **Appendix A** was 2,100 in April 1994. At most the saving might be the cost of the board or council currently governing each quango (total annual cost around £1m); but even that would partly transfer elsewhere, because the functions would still need supervision.

Reasons for Establishment of Quangos

279   As has already been mentioned, quangos have been created by Governments of both persuasions. The reasons vary in each case, but generally include one or more of the following.

The Need for Specialist Expertise

280   This is self evident in the case of most advisory bodies: their whole raison d'être is to provide specialist knowledge not available within Government. It is also an important factor with many executive bodies, from the National Library to the Sports Council to the business expertise required on the Welsh Development Agency.

The Need for Greater Impetus

281   Quangos are sometimes created when Ministers want to give a higher profile or a push to a particular area of Government activity. Quango chairmen can speak out and promote the functions of the quango more publicly than civil servants; and can devote much more time and energy to the task than can Ministers. Of the 19 executive bodies listed in **Appendix A**, 13 have salaried chairmen devoting two to three days per week to running a quango and nine have salaried deputy chairmen. With the right appointments, these quangos can be strongly led by their boards. They can do so within a framework of tight accountability and control. The Welsh Executive can continue to issue strategic guidance letters and to require quangos to submit their corporate and operational plans for specific approval, as Ministers do now.

Operational Effectiveness and Financial Freedom

282   These considerations apply mainly to economic development agencies such as the Welsh Development Agency and Land Authority for Wales. They are less circumscribed than Government departments by the Treasury's detailed rules of Government accounting. When attracting inward investment they can clinch deals much faster than can local authorities with their committee structure or Whitehall with its extensive processes of consultation.

Involvement of Private and Voluntary Sectors

283   Both central and local government have experimented with non-elected bodies as a way of encouraging private sector companies, banks and the voluntary sector to tackle environmental problems, housing, economic decline and urban regeneration. For the public sector agencies the concern is to get access to private sector funds and expertise. The private sector is reluctant to join partnerships which are wholly controlled by politicians, national or local. For effective public/private sector partnerships intermediary bodies are often required, in which all partners can feel they have a stake.

Artistic and Cultural Freedom

284 It is a long-standing bi-partisan policy that artistic and cultural freedom are better protected if funding decisions are taken at one remove from Government. Similar considerations apply to the National Library and National Museum of Wales, and (outside the sponsorship of the Welsh Office) to the BBC and S4C.

Professional Regulation and Training

285 This applies mainly in the health field, where the Government is a monopoly purchaser of the services of doctors, dentists, nurses and midwives, but these are largely self-regulating professions which set their own standards of entry and training. The advisory committees on post-graduate medical education, etc. provide a forum in which Government and the profession can meet to discuss future numbers, professional standards and other issues of mutual concern.

Reducing the Risk of Corruption

286 An example in the political field is the Local Government Boundary Commission. It cannot prevent electoral gerrymandering; but it offers independent advice, and when the Government departs from that advice it has to offer reasons, so that the process is exposed to public scrutiny. In the economic field the main risk areas are industrial grants and the granting of planning permission. Although there have been financial scandals in the Welsh quangos few have concerned the award or withholding of grants. In local government in Wales instances of fraud and corruption continue to be uncovered, serving as a reminder that democratic accountability is not necessarily a guarantee of clean government.

Decentralisation of Decision Making

287 The same arguments which are advanced for devolving power away from London also apply within Wales. Those who argue for all decisions in Wales to be given to the Welsh Assembly risk overloading the Assembly and the politicians in it. Although democratically elected, they will not have a monopoly of wisdom: to exercise power effectively they must be willing to share it.

Different Degrees of Independence for Different Quangos

288 The preceding paragraphs have examined the role and function of quangos in order to correct the simplistic assumption that the Welsh Executive can or should take over all or most quango functions. In most cases the role of the Executive and Assembly will be to provide strong democratic control and oversight. The Executive may set the policy and financial framework, but should not feel obliged to provide the services itself. The Assembly can approve the policy objectives, and call chairmen and chief executives to account for their performance.

289 The new Welsh Executive will need to conduct a review of quangos to develop a proper framework of democratic control. Subject to improvements to the appointments process (discussed at paragraphs 273 to 276 above), most of the advisory bodies can be left as they are: they are not the cause of public concern. Concern focuses on the executive bodies listed in **Appendix A.** Here the review will need to decide on:
- direct control or need for a separate board.
- transfer to local government.
- appointments procedures.
- remuneration of appointed members.
- scrutiny of key appointments by the Assembly.

- annual reporting arrangements.
- audit arrangements.
- accountability to:
  - Ministers
  - the Assembly
  - other stakeholders
  - the general public.
- requirements of openness and transparency.
- admission of the press and public to meetings.
- setting performance targets and monitoring performance.
- sanctions for poor performance.

290 There is no need for a uniform solution: but there is a need for greater consistency over appointments procedures, annual reporting and audit arrangements (which is something the Government has recognised in its response to the Nolan Committee's report). There also needs to be a general culture of transparency. Within such a framework the range of policy choices for different quangos can be shown in the following illustrative models:

- **Direct control:** service provided direct by the Welsh Executive. Casework dealt with by officials; difficult cases referred to the Executive Member. Executive Member answerable to the Assembly about the policy and individual cases.
- **Low independence:** separate board appointed by the Executive Member. Tight framework agreement and performance targets, little operational discretion. Tight budget. National Audit Office audit.
- **Medium independence:** separate board, some appointed by Executive, some nominated by outside bodies. Looser performance targets, greater operational discretion. 100% publicly funded. National Audit Office audit.
- **High independence:** TEC boards appoint their own members. Board sets its own performance targets, some approved by Executive. Substantially publicly funded but also attracts outside funds. Independent auditors.

291 These are for illustration only and do not exhaust all the possibilities. Nor should the range be thought of as a single continuum on the scale of dependence / independence. Finance is a separate variable: a body might have significant operational freedom (as do the TECs) but be subject to tight financial control. Also for illustration only is the application of the criteria in paragraphs 279 to 285 to the executive bodies in **Appendix A.** The last column of the table records some of the factors which suggest that the body might need to retain a degree of independence.

292 None of this is scientific; it is a question of balancing the need for greater public accountability and scrutiny against the operational requirements of each NDPB. Ultimately it is a political judgement where the balance is struck. **Appendix A** merely sets out some of the considerations to illustrate which organisations might need to maintain a degree of independence in order to retain specialist expertise, preserve cultural or professional independence, manage commercial operations and engage with outside partners.

Scrutiny by the Assembly

293 None of this need prevent the Assembly maintaining close oversight of quangos and subjecting them to regular scrutiny. It could debate the framework agreements under which the quangos operate and require Executive Members to explain the policy objectives and targets which they

have set. The Assembly is likely to set up specialist committees in most of the subject areas in which the main executive bodies operate (economic development; education; arts and culture). Like Westminster's select committees, the committees could call the chairmen and chief officers to appear before them and give an account of their performance and their future plans. The committees could also hold enquiries into particular cases. And with certain key appointments the committees could invite the chairman designate to appear and answer questions about his or her suitability for the post before the Executive Member confirms the appointment.

Transfer to Local Government

294   In a restructuring of quangos not all functions need to be retained at an all-Wales level. Some quangos were established to take over functions carried out by local government, and those functions could in theory be returned to local government. There would need to be proper enquiry in each case along the lines proposed above; the conclusion might be that in each case all-Wales functions or values would be lost. The most likely candidates for possible transfer to local authorities would be:

- the funding responsibilities of Tai Cymru to the housing departments of local authorities; but it or a successor body would need to remain as the regulatory authority for housing associations in Wales.
- funding for further education could transfer from the Further Education Funding Council to the education departments of local authorities; but the functions of monitoring quality, assisting mergers and rationalising provision might need to be retained at the centre.
- funding for TECs was formerly a central government function, which could be transferred to local government; or their boards could be reconstituted to include local authority representatives while the funding continued to come from the Welsh administration.

295   The TECs might also be considered alongside the Wesh Development Agency, on the lines of the relationship between the LECs in Scotland and Scottish Enterprise. The merits of these proposals would need to be carefully explored in each case; but they could offer another means of bringing the functions of certain quangos under tighter democratic control.

NHS Bodies

296   This is another area which deserves separate study. How NHS bodies might fit into a revised framework of accountability depends on wider decisions about the future of NHS Trusts and GP fundholders, and the role of DHAs and FHSAs as combined purchasing agencies after April 1996. It also depends on the role of local authorities, who would like to be represented again on the boards of DHAs; and some of whom would like to see local government resuming the lead role in community health and public health. There needs to be stronger local accountability within the NHS; and at regional level accountability can be through the Assembly. The Assembly will probably want to establish a health committee to scrutinise the quality of health care across Wales; but delivery of health services would remain the responsibility of the Executive and whatever structures it puts in place at district and local level.

The Welsh Language

297   The Welsh language merits separate mention because of its special place in the Welsh political landscape. Where previously there had been an advisory body, the statutory Welsh Language Board was established under the Welsh Language Act 1993 with the primary function of

promoting and facilitating the use of the Welsh language. It ensures that all public bodies prepare language schemes embodying policy statements relating to the provision of Welsh language services, along with associated practical arrangements and timetables, in accordance with guidelines approved by Parliament. The Board also provides advice to the Secretary of State and others on the use of the language, on the principle that in the conduct of public business and the administration of justice in Wales, the English and Welsh language should be treated on the basis of equality. The Welsh Executive would assume the powers of the Secretary of State to appoint members of the Welsh Language Board; and as the leading public body in Wales the Assembly would need to be scrupulous in respecting the equality of the two languages.

Conclusion

298 Quangos remain the subject of public concern in Wales because of their inadequate accountability; the nature of the people appointed to their boards; and lapses in their internal management. But it is only a few high profile executive bodies which have given rise to that concern. The majority of quangos are specialist bodies which seldom come to notice, operating in technical fields where the Government needs independent expertise and advice, which is generally freely given.

299 The creation of a Welsh Assembly will provide the opportunity to review the whole framework and accountability structure. In many areas there are sound reasons for retaining quangos with a degree of operational independence. This can be illustrated by sorting quangos into different categories, depending on the degree of specialist expertise, outside impetus, operational freedom, involvement of other partners, artistic freedom and professional independence which is required.

300 A review of the appointments process has already been carried out by the Nolan Committee. If in future the Welsh Executive follows the Nolan Committee's recommended code of practice and the Assembly maintains close scrutiny of quangos' performance and operations, much of the concern about quangos could be laid to rest.

Chapter 9

Relations with Local Government and with Europe

Introduction

301 The Assembly will need to establish effective working relations with all the other levels of government. Relations with central government were examined in chapter 7. The first part of this chapter considers relations between the Assembly and local government; and the second part the Assembly's relations with Europe.

Local Government: A Difficult Relationship

302 Relations with local government start from a low base. There has been continual interference by central government with the powers, functions, structures and funding of local government coupled with significant centralisation of power. The relationship has been largely defined by central government rather than being based on any concept of partnership. There has been little effective consultation with local authorities in the setting of policies, priorities and financial targets, many of which have simply been imposed.

303 Local government will be one of the functions transferred to the Assembly and the Welsh administration, so that the new administration has the potential to be every bit as dominant as the Welsh Office has been. Local government interests came out strongly against the proposed Assembly in the 1979 referendum. It is fortunate that the Welsh County Councils and the Association of Welsh Districts have since declared themselves in favour, because attitudes may harden again unless safeguards are included to protect the position of local government. This chapter considers what legal and institutional safeguards might be required. The need for such safeguards is not wholly fanciful: experience in Europe shows that the development of regional government is often at the expense of local government. This should not come as a surprise. New political institutions want to carve out power for themselves; and regional governments can interfere in the activities of local authorities on their doorstep and pursue local quarrels in a way which remote central governments cannot.

304 The main points of friction are likely to be:
- **finance:** the Welsh administration will take on responsibility for distributing block grant to local authorities, and will decide the quantum and the formula - both highly vexed issues.
- **local government reorganisation:** at the time of the recent local government reorganisation the Labour Party pledged a further review of local government. The same pledge was made in the 1970s. Local government may have little enthusiasm for any further reorganisation.
- **strategic direction:** the administration will exercise powers of strategic direction and control over such issues as strategic and land use planning, roads and transport, schools curriculum, economic development, specialist resources for social services and education departments. The capacity of the new unitary authorities to deliver some of these major strategic services has already been called in question, even through joint arrangements. If these arrangements do not work the administration will be tempted to take over the services.
- **raising standards:** service standards may be at risk as the 22 new unitary authorities come to terms with their new responsibilities in highways, transport, social services and specialist education. The Assembly and Welsh administration may need to lay down minimum standards, and so will assume the mantle of the present Government in the drive to raise national standards for local services.

Towards a Better Relationship

305 The basic principles for developing a more harmonious relationship must include:
- **agreement about the boundaries between the Assembly and local government:** the role of the Assembly and the Welsh administration will be to set the framework and minimum national standards within which local government operates. Within that framework it will be a matter for local authorities to determine service delivery arrangements and their internal structures.
- **stability about the functions of local government:** to help their new organisational structures to bed down the new unitary authorities need to have a period of stability of three to five years secure in the knowledge that their functions and responsibilities will remain unchanged.
- **agreement about the system of local government finance:** finance is at the root of the difficulties which bedevil the central/local relationship. In the aftermath of the poll tax, and the introduction of the uniform business rate local government in Wales is dependent upon central government for 85% of its income. To restore local accountability this proportion must be reduced. And in the aftermath of local government reorganisation there may need to be a fundamental review of the Standard Spending Assessment formula by which block grant is distributed, to provide a better match to the spending needs of the new unitary authorities.

306 All this will require considerable self-denial on the part of the Welsh administration. Assuming that legislation to create a Welsh Assembly is introduced following the next general election, the new Assembly and administration will not come into being until two to three years after the new unitary authorities come into force in April 1996. There will be all sorts of teething troubles, major and minor scandals and inefficiencies exposed as the new arrangements settle down. And the pressures to squeeze further efficiency savings out of local government will be very powerful. The new Government will be under the same intense budgetary pressures as the present one; and every pound passed onto local government will be a pound less for the administration to spend on its own services.

307 Nor should it be thought that Government interference is always counter-productive. Although the introduction of compulsory competitive tendering was bitterly resented by local authorities, independent research for the Joseph Rowntree Foundation has shown that it has delivered significant efficiency gains. One officer interviewed reflected the conclusions of the report:
> *"the benefits were we saved money and the services were no worse. Broadly it is the same service at less cost. But we would never have done it without compulsion..."*[48]

308 Another research study for the Joseph Rowntree Foundation has underlined the stability and consensus in Welsh local government. Urban and industrial South Wales and North East Wales have long been dominated by the Labour Party:
> *"There are not the periodic changes of electoral fortune and hence changes of Council membership found in many parts of England. Therefore Councillors tend to grow old in waiting for death to offer the release that may elsewhere be found in electoral defeat".*[49]

The report of the Widdicombe Committee of Enquiry into the Conduct of Local Authority Business in 1986 found that 54% of Welsh councillors were over 60, compared with 20% in England; and 95% of Welsh councillors were male compared with 80% in England. Given this background it is perhaps not surprising that much of Welsh local government is strongly traditional in its outlook.

How to Achieve a Better Relationship

309 The justification for intervention may often be strong; and the pressures and temptations to intervene will be intense. Despite this the new administration and Assembly must resist. If there is to develop a more effective and harmonious relationship persuasion not compulsion must be the order of the day. This can be buttressed by a number of legal and institutional pillars to help keep the relationship on a sound footing.

Legal Recognition of Local Government

310 In Scotland it has been suggested the legislation should embody the principle of subsidiarity to ensure the Scottish Parliament does not suck up powers from local government. Others look for salvation to ratification of the European Charter of Local Self Government. Neither source is likely to yield a justiciable set of principles which Welsh local authorities can pray in aid. But it might be worth including in the legislation an obligation on the Assembly to maintain a strong and effective system of local government.

A Protocol or Compact with Local Government

311 This seems likely to be a more effective and productive road to follow. The protocol could cover the respective responsibilities of each tier and the criteria to be observed when considering any changes; and provide for a right of local government to be consulted on all legislative proposals, to make submissions to the Assembly and to promote legislation.

Representation on Assembly Committees

312 Local authorities themselves have power to co-opt outsiders onto their committees. Their Education Committees have co-opted members by statute; and some local authorities have co-opted representatives of the local Chamber of Commerce onto the economic development committee. The advantages are that it can broaden the debate, and introduce outside expertise; and a small Assembly will have relatively few members to cover quite a large area of subject committees. The arguments against are that co-option might dilute the legitimacy of the elected body; and there is a risk of co-opting old friends rather than independent experts. Perhaps for these reasons the 1978 Act did not include a power to co-opt.

313 If there is no power to co-opt the Assembly could establish a joint liaison committee with local government. If there is power to co-opt, and if there are subject committees which parallel the portfolios of the Executive Members, the obvious committee onto which to co-opt local authority members would be the local government committee. But it would make sense to consider local authority representation also on the committees covering education; transport; planning and the environment; health; and finance. The local authority members should have speaking but not voting rights.

Dual Mandate

314 Another way of strengthening links between the two tiers would be to encourage Councillors to stand for election to the Assembly. Plaid Cymru proposes direct representation of local government in the Assembly by having an upper chamber (the Congress) composed of two representatives from each of the 22 unitary authorities. A bicameral Assembly might be thought excessive for a country of three million people (although Stormont had a Senate) and there may be other ways of promoting strong links. Membership of the Assembly is unlikely to be a full-time occupation (see Chapter 6), so that it would be feasible for someone to be a member of a

local authority and the Assembly. But it might not to be encouraged by the political parties: Labour Party rules did not permit membership of a County and a District Council. Interestingly this prohibition helps to illustrate the value of dual membership: relations between Cardiff City Council and South Glamorgan County Council were generally more strained when both were under Labour control than when one was under Tory control - as the Tories allowed overlapping membership.

Timing of Elections

315 This raises a further point about the timing of elections to the Assembly and their phasing in relation to local government elections. Should the elections be co-ordinated, or should the elections for one be held in the mid-term of the other? The arguments for holding elections at the same time are that both bodies would be elected on the same political tide, which might help to ensure harmonious relations; there would be higher voter turnout, and less risk of voter fatigue; and reduced cost. The arguments against are that local government might prefer a separate date to avoid the local government elections being clouded by wider issues; and mid-term elections might create a check and balance between the two tiers.

Finance

316 The Welsh administration will want to continue the regular forum (The Welsh Consultative Council on Local Government Finance) in which the Secretary of State currently meets local government to discuss spending needs and the grant distribution formula. A revised formula is urgently needed, because the application of the old formula to the new unitary authorities has thrown up serious anomalies, leading to huge council tax increases in some authorities. The Welsh Office is committed to reviewing the formula, which may be revised by the time the Assembly is created. If not it will be one of the first challenges facing the new Welsh administration. Another test will be whether the administration restores the non-domestic rate to local authorities and removes capping powers.

Wales in Europe

317 The influence of Europe on UK policy and law has increased enormously since devolution was last considered in the 1970s. EC law impacts on all areas of government activity; and the Maastricht Treaty introduced new powers for the EC in the areas of education, industry, culture and transport and communications. In 1988 Jacques Delors, the then President of the European Commission, estimated that by 1998 at least 80% of all economic and social legislation in the member states would be coming from Europe. In areas like agriculture and environmental regulation that is already the case; and in many respects the Welsh economy is more dependent upon decisions made in Brussels than in London. One of the key tests facing the Welsh Assembly and administration will be how to maximise Welsh influence in Europe, to ensure that Wales' voice is heard and Welsh interests strongly represented.

The Present System of Representing Wales in Europe

318 The basic starting point must be the recognition that the UK is the representative member state. This factor shapes all of the current relationships which Wales and Welsh institutions and bodies (central/local government, quangos, academic institutions, the voluntary sector) maintain with the European Union.

319   This is particularly evident in the key decision making forum of the Union, the Council of Ministers, where Government Ministers from each member state meet in order to make the key policy and budgetary decisions. The Secretary of State for Wales has no right to attend, and rarely does so. Welsh interests are normally represented by the Secretaries of State for Employment, Agriculture, Environment, etc.

320   Wales has five MEPs. They are directly elected by the 'first past the post' electoral system and serve for 5 years. The European Parliament has to be consulted on decisions and policies but the final decision generally rests with the Council of Ministers. Whilst the 1996 Intergovernmental Conference (IGC) will almost certainly be asked to give stronger direct powers to the Parliament there is little sign that the member state Governments will accede to this.

321   The Committee of the Regions, which was introduced following the Maastricht Treaty, represents a recognition of the increasing importance of regional government in most European Union states. Wales has three representatives on the Committee. These are local authority members representing the Labour, Conservative and Plaid Cymru parties, nominated by the Secretary of State. The Committee of the Regions has only a consultative role, and this is also unlikely to change following the IGC.

322   The main day to day administrative contact for Wales with the European Commission is through the relevant Whitehall departments whose representation in Brussels is handled by the UK Permanent Representation to the European Commission. This is part of the FCO staffed by secondees from various Government departments, including in recent years a secondee from the Welsh Office. The Whitehall departments with lead responsibilities for European matters of most vital importance for Wales include Agriculture, Education and Employment, Environment and Industry. In these policy areas, Welsh organisations wishing to influence and inform EU policy must do so via Whitehall.

323   The Welsh Office has prime responsibility for certain crucial aspects of EU regional policy in Wales, in particular the regional structural fund programmes. The Welsh Office has retained tightly centralised control of these funds. In March 1996, the Secretary of State announced the creation of a new executive to manage the European structural funds under the guidance of a partnership of regional economic development organisations including local authorities.

324   In recent years, a large number of regional representative offices have become established in Brussels which seek to strengthen the contacts between regional and local governments and the European Commission. Wales was in the forefront of this move with the Welsh local authorities, Welsh Development Agency, Welsh Tourist Board, Development Board for Rural Wales, University of Wales and TECs coming together to establish the Wales European Centre (WEC) in 1992. The WEC is essentially an intelligence and information exchange rather than a lobbying organisation.

Deficiencies of the Present System

325   Complaints about the present system fall in three areas: lack of a coherent voice; centralisation; and access to funding. The Council may conduct its business without any consideration of, or direct consultation on, the needs of the regions. This deficiency is not unique to the UK regions; but it must be recognised that Wales' interests can easily become subsumed in the consideration of wider UK interests.

326 The Committee of the Regions is subject to a gross mismatch in the status of members and the resources provided to support them. The Welsh members, elected as local authority councillors for their wards, sit alongside senior European regional presidents and prime ministers. Whereas the German, Spanish and French members of the Committee of the Regions have been elected to their positions in order to carry out coherent regional functions, the Welsh members have been nominated by the Secretary of State on the basis of the need for 'balance' in political representation. The Welsh members of the Committee of the Regions do not represent a coherent electorate or body in Wales.

327 The Wales European Centre is often mentioned as a vital link for Wales with the EU. However, the voice of the WEC is not representative of any single elected body of opinion: it is only a partial and unofficial voice. The main governmental contact between Wales and the European Commission is via the UK Permanent Representation in Brussels (UKRep). The Welsh local authorities, public bodies and the private sector organisations have all attempted to establish regular contacts and policy discussions directly with the EC. As a result there has been friction between these Welsh organisations and central government at both Whitehall and Welsh Office levels.

328 In directing funding into the Welsh economy from Europe there is a tension between the demands of UK Government policy and those of Wales as one of Europe's 'less favoured' regions. This was classically seen in the decisions made by the UK Government on Assisted Area status in the UK, followed by the decision made by the EC to deny Objective 1 status to Wales. Similarly in the area of structural funds, the basis for the allocation is determined by the EC in negotiation with the UK Government, with Welsh Office Ministers being junior partners in these negotiations. Welsh Office Ministers may lead on Welsh regional structural fund programmes, but always within parameters set by the DTI.

Representing Welsh Interests after Devolution

329 It is tempting to think all this will change with the creation of a Welsh Assembly. But the institutional structures and fundamental power relationships in Europe will remain essentially the same. The member state will be the UK; and Welsh and Scottish interests will continue to be represented through UK Ministers and departments. Suggestions that a Welsh Assembly might lead to direct representation in the Council of Ministers are wishful thinking. The Welsh administration and Assembly will have to work through the UK structures which will continue to be the main vehicle for voicing Wales' concerns.

330 It is instructive to study the experience of other member states with regional governments. In Spain the autonomous regions sought to negotiate a co-operation agreement with the national government but have failed to gain the influence over EU policy they desired. The Belgian and German regions have done better, but they are federal systems which confer areas of exclusive legislative competence upon the regions. The Belgian regions have a co-operation agreement with the federal government laying down the composition of the Council of Ministers delegation and the decision rules concerning negotiation strategy and voting. The German Länder have formalised rights recognised in the new Article 23 of the German constitution which provides that a representative of the Länder may be included in the German delegation when matters affecting the exclusive legislative competencies of the Länder are being discussed.

331 The important point to note for Wales is that the regional and national governments in other member states have negotiated formal agreements. So here the existing machinery which consists of internal arrangements within Whitehall will need to be formalised into an external one between governments within the same state. The agreement need not be enshrined in legislation (in Germany it was initially recorded in an exchange of letters); but the Welsh Assembly legislation should contain a requirement that the two Governments enter into a co-operation agreement on European affairs. The content of the agreement would be a matter for negotiation, but as a minimum it might contain:

- the right to send officials as observers to any working group meetings where matters devolved to Wales are being discussed; and to participate fully in preparatory meetings of the UK delegation.

- a similar right for Welsh Executive Members to attend preparatory meetings.

- the establishment of an intergovernmental committee at official level to co-ordinate European policy in areas transferred to Wales. In practice this might simply be the existing committees within the Cabinet Office structure, reformulated to call them 'intergovernmental'.

- the right to continue to receive full reports from UKRep on all EU business relating to matters transferred to Wales.

- rights to a share of UK representation in the European Parliament and the Committee of the Regions, and to nominate suitable candidates for the other major European institutions (the Commissioners, the European Court of Justice, the Economic and Social Committee; and the staff of the European institutions).

- observer status at any Inter-Governmental Conference called to revise the Community treaties (a right granted to the German Länder in advance of the Maastricht negotiations).

- agreement to maintain secondments from the Welsh Office to UKRep.

332 Two points are worth drawing out further. First, it is in the interests of both the Welsh and UK Governments that Welsh officials should be fully involved in the development and negotiation of policy in certain key areas where they have particular expertise e.g. hill farming, support for minority languages, inward investment from Japan. Second, the political sensitivities of involving Welsh Executive Members in UK Cabinet committees should not be under-estimated, particularly under different administrations in Cardiff and London. If this is acceptable under similar administrations in both capitals then it should be written into the agreement. If it is not acceptable, even from the start, then the agreement should specify procedures for invoking an inter-Ministerial committee where Welsh officials feel the debate needs to be moved to that level.

The Role of the Welsh Assembly

333 It is a consequence of the Council of Ministers being a forum for negotiation between Governments that national parliaments for the most part find themselves insufficiently involved in the negotiating process. The phenomenon extends also to regional Assemblies. It is frequently remarked, for example, that the increased involvement of the Länder in German policy making has been won by the Länder governments, but has not extended to their parliaments.

334 This might turn out to be the case for the Welsh Assembly too. To prevent its marginalisation it will need to adopt procedures which give it the best possible opportunity to hold the Welsh Executive to account for actions in the European field. The Assembly might include in its procedures a number of elements building on existing Westminster practice for the monitoring of European affairs:

- a debate on the UK Government's policy in advance of every European Council.
- the same service as Westminster in terms of documentation, written reports of Council meetings, perhaps even repetition of Ministerial statements with a suitable commentary by the relevant Welsh Executive Member.
- parallel powers to scrutinise EC legislation - with the option of asking for a debate in Westminster, or making a report to the Commons or Lords Scrutiny Committee in the event of disquiet.
- liaison with the Scrutiny Committees in other member states' parliaments for the exchange of information and best practice.
- if the IGC agrees further measures for inter-parliamentary co-operation, the Welsh Assembly should participate.

Liaison with Welsh MEPs

335 Wales will continue to be represented by five MEPs. Devolution should be used to integrate them more closely into the political process in Wales. The Welsh Assembly should welcome the five Welsh MEPs and seek their active collaboration in building up its relations with the European Parliament and the Community, in a way never achieved by Westminster. They should be allowed full access to the Assembly building and its facilities; and the Assembly should consider co-opting Welsh MEPs onto its European Affairs Committee - to encourage the flow of information and to assist in early warning as well as scrutiny of EC legislation. The Welsh Executive will also want to liaise as necessary with Welsh MEPs to maximise their usefulness in influencing legislative proposals.

Official Representation in Brussels

336 At present the Wales European Centre is a partnership between a wide range of Welsh organisations. The choices for the Welsh Assembly will be:
1. to establish a new office in Brussels.
2. to restructure the WEC to make it an agency of the Assembly.
3. to participate in the WEC like any other client.
On grounds of cost and continuity options 2 or 3 seem more sensible. Either will provide a base in Brussels for the Assembly and its members to gain direct access to the Community institutions and, more importantly, to gain from the intelligence gathering which the office already undertakes on behalf of its clients. But a change in the WEC's status as a loose partnership transmitting information between Wales and Brussels into a more focused 'lobbying' office would need to be agreed by all partners. It is by no means certain that they would willingly surrender this facility to the control of an Assembly; nor is it certain that the Assembly and the other partners would be able to agree on the matters or policies which a WEC adopting a lobbying role would be required to handle with UKRep and the European Commission.

337 For the Welsh Executive the main source of representation will be via UKRep. A co-operation agreement should ensure continuity of the information flows; and the Welsh administration should ensure continuation of the arrangements whereby one of its officials is seconded to UKRep. It will not need its own representative office.

Committee of the Regions

338 Formally members of the Committee of the Regions will still need to be nominated by the member state; but nominees could come from the Assembly rather than Welsh local government. The Welsh Executive will need to decide whether to nominate one or more Executive Members, to sit alongside the political leaders of the other European regions; and

107

whether to seek party balance by inviting a representative of the main opposition parties. The Assembly will also need to negotiate with the Welsh local authorities, who will be reluctant to relinquish their current representation on the Committee of the Regions. A possible compromise would be to limit Assembly representation to two members with a third place left for local authority nomination.

Conclusion

339   Central/local government relations are at a low ebb. There is great potential for the Assembly and Welsh administration to play a more constructive role, and the new unitary authorities will need strategic support. The key to developing harmonious relationships lies in respecting the boundaries between the Assembly and local government; allowing for a period of stability for the new unitary structures to bed down; and reaching a new agreement about the system of local government finance. This would be greatly helped if there was a protocol or compact covering the respective powers of each tier, and consultative and other procedures; co-option of local authority members onto relevant Assembly committees; and dual membership permitting Councillors to stand for the Assembly without having to resign from their local authorities.

340   Europe will continue to have a significant impact on life in Wales. The Welsh Assembly and administration will want to maximise Welsh influence in Brussels. This will continue to be done through UK Ministers and departments because the UK is the member state. To secure adequate representation of Welsh interests, the Welsh Executive will need to negotiate a co-operation agreement with the UK Government providing for a continuing flow of information, participation in preparatory meetings, and the right to send officials and Executive Members as observers to working group and Council meetings on devolved matters.

341   The Welsh Assembly will need to establish the same procedures for monitoring, debate and scrutiny as have been established at Westminster. It should welcome the five Welsh MEPs and co-opt them onto its Welsh European Affairs Committee. In terms of permanent representation in Brussels, the Welsh executive can continue to use UKRep; the Welsh Assembly can join the Wales European Centre, but must not prejudice the service provided to the other partners.

Chapter 10

Finance

Introduction

342 Stable funding arrangements will be crucial to the devolution settlement. Most of the debate in Wales about finance has focused on the immediate impact on public expenditure: will the additional cost of the Assembly be £15m, £50m or £100m per annum? This question will be examined in chapter 13. The figures are not unimportant, but they are insignificant in comparison with total Government expenditure in Wales.

343 It is the totals which we need to look at first, because the whole system for determining public expenditure in Wales may need to change post-devolution. The current funding arrangements are based upon a largely unquestioned internal allocation mechanism within Government. This may not survive the transition to what in future will be an external transfer mechanism between separate administrations.

Government Expenditure in Wales

344 In January 1996 the Welsh Office published for the first time figures for general government expenditure allocated to Wales. Total Government expenditure for Wales is estimated to have been £14.7bn in 1993-94. This was 5.2% of the UK total, slightly above the proportion of the UK population which lives in Wales (5%). Expenditure per head on Wales was £5,040 compared with the UK average of £4,871.

345 Total tax receipts raised in Wales in 1993-94 are estimated by the Welsh Office to have been £9.3bn (4% of total UK receipts). The Government's figures thus show that Wales has a substantial structural budget deficit. Total Government expenditure in 1993-94 on behalf of Welsh residents exceeded tax revenues raised in Wales by £5.3bn.

346 Although the year was one of recession the overall conclusion is inescapable. They demonstrate the unreality of any proposals which suggest that the new Welsh Government might be self-financing. For the foreseeable future a devolved Government in Wales will continue to rely on block funding from the British Exchequer, and needs to have a keen understanding of how the block is calculated.

The Barnett Formula and the Welsh Block

347 The territorial breakdown of general Government expenditure (GGE) divides it into identifiable and non-identifiable expenditure. Non-identifiable GGE is expenditure such as defence which is incurred on behalf of the UK as a whole; it amounts to some 26% of the total. Identifiable GGE covers expenditure undertaken in providing services for the residents of a territory. In 1993-94 total identifiable GGE allocated to Wales was £11.4bn. £4.5bn of this was social security expenditure, administered throughout the UK by the Department of Social Security; and only £6.3bn came under the budget of the Secretary of State for Wales.

348 97% of Welsh Office expenditure comes within the 'Welsh block'. Unlike the other Whitehall spending departments, the territorial departments (including Scotland and Northern Ireland) do not engage in detailed annual negotiations with the Treasury. Changes to their budgets are

calculated by means of a formula based upon changes accruing to comparable programmes in England - the 'Barnett formula'. This derives from a Treasury study undertaken in the 1970s in anticipation of devolution. It concluded that, taking data from 1976-77, the relative amounts of expenditure per capita required to provided "the same range and levels of service as in England" for a range of services proposed for devolution were as follows (actual spending levels in brackets)[50]:

Table 8 Barnett's Needs Assessment Study 1976–77			
England	**Scotland**	**Wales**	**Northern Ireland**
100 (100)	116 (122)	109 (106)	131 (135)

349 It will be noted that expenditure in Wales at the time for the services concerned fell below the Treasury's estimate of Welsh expenditure needs; but the per capita figures available from 1960 onwards suggested Scotland had persistently received more than its estimated needs. The then Chief Secretary to the Treasury, Joel Barnett, set about devising a system to remedy these defects. His chosen method was to ensure that any future changes in the Scottish budget should be calculated as a proportion of the changes in equivalent English spending. Basing this percentage on relative shares of population in 1976, Barnett deemed that for every £85 *change* in expenditure on comparable English services, Wales should receive £5 and Scotland £10. Scotland thus gained 11.76% of any change in English spending and Wales 5.88%.

350 The Barnett formula was designed to introduce order into the setting of Scottish and Welsh budgets. If public expenditure had continued to rise the per capita expenditure figures would gradually have moved closer, reducing Scotland and Wales' provision relative to England. This convergence does not appear to have been realised. Scotland's population has fallen both absolutely and relative to England, undermining the convergence bias; and the squeeze on public spending through the 1980s meant that the changes in the English budget were not dramatic, so that the cumulative effect of the formula on changes in relative spending was limited. In view of this history, the then Chief Secretary, Michael Portillo revised the formula in 1992 to reflect Scotland's smaller share of the UK's population. The revised formula guarantees Scotland only 10.66% of changes in comparable English expenditure, and increases Wales' share from 5.88% to 6.02%.

351 Identifiable GGE per head in Wales continues to be higher than the UK average, but below the levels in Scotland and Northern Ireland:

Table 9   Identifiable General Government Expenditure Per Head by Territory

	1990-91	1991-92	1992-93	1993-94	£ per head 1994-95
England	2,611	2,983	3,210	3,410	3,634
Scotland	3,204	3,520	3,951	4,227	4,505
Northern Ireland	3,858	4,213	4,503	4,778	4,976
Wales	2,957	3,290	3,796	4,020	4,208
UK	2,715	3,080	3,341	3,551	3,760

Identifiable General Government Expenditure Per Head Relative to England

	1990-91	1991-92	1992-93	1993-94	Index (England = 100) 1994-95
England	100	100	100	100	100
Scotland	123	118	123	124	124
Northern Ireland	148	148	141	140	137
Wales	113	110	118	118	116

Source: HM Treasury, Public Expenditure Statistical Analyses 1996-97 (Table 7.1), March 1996, Cm 3201.

352 These aggregate figures for identifiable GGE conceal some interesting variations in spending between the different major services:

Table 10 Identifiable General Government Expenditure Per Head on Major Services 1994-5

	Index (United Kingdom identifiable expenditure = 100)			
	England	Scotland	Wales	Northern Ireland
Agriculture, fisheries, food and forestry	76	192	173	382
Trade, industry, energy and employment	83	168	138	313
Transport	101	105	95	64
Housing	88	171	149	160
Other environmental services	93	132	157	107
Law, order and protective services	95	105	71	273
Education	96	126	99	136
Health and personal social services	97	122	109	110
Social security	98	108	113	113
Total expenditure on services	96	120	112	132
Rebased England = 100	100	124	116	137

Source: HM Treasury, Public Expenditure Statistical Analyses 1996-97 (Table 7.6B), March 1996, Cm 3201.

353 The biggest services in expenditure terms are social security (£89bn in 1994-95), health and social services (£46bn), and education (£36bn). Social security spending in Wales is relatively high because of her relative poverty: in 1993 the index of GDP per capita in Wales stood at 84.7, while in Scotland it had reached 98.4 (UK = 100). Spending in Scotland on health and education is markedly higher than in both England and Wales. These identifiable GGE figures, based to England = 100 **(Table 9)**, suggest that actual levels of spending in Scotland and Wales were higher than their relative expenditure needs as assessed in 1976-77 **(Table 8)**.

Government Expenditure in Wales after Devolution

354 The political parties (including the Conservatives) continue to support the principle of equalisation on the basis of relative need. The Scottish Constitutional Convention has said "The principle of equalisation will continue. This means resources will be pooled on a UK basis and distributed on the basis of relative need."[51] The Wales Labour Party has said devolved Government in Wales would be funded through a continued form of central government grant based on a guaranteed equalisation formula.

Maintaining the Barnett Formula

355 Both the Scottish Constitutional Convention and the Wales Labour Party anticipate that the Barnett formula will continue to be used, which is understandable because it provides continuity, predictability, and a satisfactory result for Scotland and Wales. However, there are several reasons to doubt whether Barnett can survive the greater scrutiny involved in an external transfer mechanism between separate administrations. These reasons are considered below under three headings: formula bypass; the English block; and transparency. They are reasons which apply more strongly in the case of Scotland, because of the larger amounts involved (the Scottish block is double the Welsh block), and the greater apparent discrepancy between expenditure and need in Scotland. But if Barnett cannot survive a post-devolution settlement in Scotland it will not be preserved in amputated form in Wales: the same principle of equalisation will need to apply to all the territories of the UK.

Formula Bypass

356 The notion of block provision determined by formula gives an incomplete picture of Welsh Office spending. There are a number of ways in which changes in the Welsh budget bypass the formula, mainly through additional funds channelled in-year:
- **spending outside the block:** agriculture, fisheries and food are the main items. In addition there are occasional calls for additional UK-wide spending during the year (e.g. an NHS pay award) which are funded on a one-off, contingency basis, outside the formula.
- **contingency reserve:** the Welsh Office has no contingency reserve to meet unforeseen events like cleaning up after the Milford Haven oil spill, but the Treasury does.

In practice the Welsh Office has had recourse up to now to a variety of funding practices *outside the block* in order to maintain its position and its solvency. A devolved Welsh Government will need access to similar levels of flexibility.

The English Block

357   A further problem lies in identifying the 'English block': the sums and the programmes of spending in England to which the Barnett formula is to be applied. On existing published Treasury data this is impossible. The precise figures for that part of English identifiable expenditure which forms the equivalent for calculating the Welsh block are not published. This lack of definition is one means by which the Treasury maintain control of the game. Without any firm definition of the English equivalent block it is easy to make changes to the composition of the Welsh block at the margins as part of the overall annual public expenditure settlement. Nobody outside the process is any the wiser.

Transparency

358   This lack of definition may be tolerable in the context of a Whitehall public expenditure round. But the degree of Treasury control that the lack of clarity affords would not be acceptable under devolution. In order to win support and legitimacy in Wales and in England all relevant data would have to be made publicly available, and the process by which the Welsh spending allocation was then calculated would have to be made more comprehensible and visible.

Block Funding and English Equivalence

359   A final important point relating to the block grant and to the needs assessment exercise is the problem which might be caused by Governments either side of the border pursuing different policies. This is the object of the devolution exercise. But the financial arrangements need to allow for it to be possible in practice. There might be problems in applying the formula where the English equivalent disappears as a result of different spending priorities in England.

360   The point can be illustrated by a hypothetical example. Suppose that a Conservative Government in London cuts income tax, introduces tax incentives for private health insurance and reduces spending on the NHS. Under the Barnett formula this would lead automatically to a proportionate cut in the block grant for Wales; but Wales might want to retain spending on the NHS. There will have to be mechanisms in place to cope with differences between concepts of the public sector in Wales and the rest of the UK. In the longer-term as it becomes politically feasible this might mean that devolved parliaments must be given more scope - along with local government - to determine their own level of resourcing through local taxation. That possibility is considered at paragraphs 367 to 375 below.

361   The Barnett formula does not appear to have brought convergence (unless levels of need have risen in Scotland and Wales since 1979). The recalibration in 1992 was partly a recognition that convergence did not seem to be happening. Further recalibration in the future cannot be ruled out. At the very least new mechanisms will be required to make the adjustments under the circumstances of devolution to a Welsh Assembly.

Alternatives to the Barnett Formula: Needs Assessment by Independent Commission

362   The Constitution Unit's report, *Scotland's Parliament,* examines how the expenditure needs of the nations and regions of the UK might be regularly assessed as part of a post-devolution settlement. The report's conclusions are:
  - there might be a regular needs assessment exercise (perhaps once every five years) to provide relevant data as objective, fair and consistent as possible, to allow a better informed judgement about spending allocations to the devolved territories and regions of the UK.

- an independent body would be responsible for conducting the exercise. For the needs assessment to be accepted as objective, it cannot be right for one of the parties (such as the Treasury) to be responsible for determining the data provided.
- the Commission would conduct the periodic needs assessment; audit the application of the formula; and make recommendations as necessary about any adjustment in the formula. Its role would be advisory; all its decisions would be for governmental and parliamentary approval.

Could the Assembly Precept upon Local Government?

363   Local government is largely funded by external finance from the Welsh Office. In 1995-96 local authorities' revenue budget of £3bn was supported through £2bn in Welsh Office grants. £0.5bn came from non-domestic rates, and only £0.4bn was raised in council tax. With devolved government in Wales responsibility for grant support to local authorities would fall to the Welsh Executive, and would represent one of its largest heads of expenditure. If its own budget was squeezed it would be tempting in turn for the Welsh Government to squeeze rate support grant to local authorities, and rely on their capacity to increase levels of council tax to make up the difference.

364   The capacity to do this would be limited because of the high gearing involved. For every 1% cut in grant support local authorities have to increase council tax by up to 10%. The protests at the council tax increases in 1996 show the limited room for manoeuvre. But it does not invalidate the general point being made, that the Welsh Government could levy taxes by proxy through the council tax by cutting its grant to the local authorities. Without any revenue under its own control this would represent its only variable source of revenue.

365   The only other variable source of revenue would be non-domestic rates. If these were returned to local authority control - as local government has demanded - there would be a greater capacity for the Welsh Executive to precept because local authorities would have a stronger revenue base. If non-domestic rates remain determined at the centre (as now) the Welsh Executive could itself decide to increase business rates to compensate local authorities for a reduction in grant support. Here too there would be limited room for manoeuvre, because the business rate in Wales is only 10% lower than in England; but the theoretical possibility would be there.

366   This risk of the Welsh Assembly precepting on local authority revenue was one of the reasons why local government turned against the proposed Assembly in the 1970s. It is a reason why local government at the least should be looking for the Assembly to have independent revenue raising power, so that it would be less tempted to tap into their resources. What are the main options?

Revenue Raising Powers

367   The fact that Welsh expenditure at present is financed for the most part through block funding from Westminster can obscure the fact that a large proportion of this revenue was raised originally in Wales. Plaid Cymru have suggested that the Welsh Senedd should be financed simply by retaining all its own tax revenue with a contribution to the UK Government to finance all-UK services.

368 This was the approach adopted for financing Stormont, the devolved Parliament established in Northern Ireland in 1920. Stormont was originally assigned all revenues raised in the province from which it was required to pay an Imperial Contribution to cover the cost of services retained at Westminster (foreign affairs, defence, etc.) with the remainder at the disposal of the Northern Ireland parliament to spend as it saw fit. But it soon became apparent that tax yields in the province were too small to finance a level of service comparable to that in the rest of the UK and adjustments had to be made. In time the Imperial Contribution became negative: the UK Exchequer contributed to the provision of services in Northern Ireland rather than receiving a contribution for central services. In 1938 the financial arrangements were recast under the Simon Declaration which promised that the UK would make good any deficit in Northern Ireland so as to guarantee services of a UK standard in the province. This also considerably constrained Stormont's scope to pursue policies different from the rest of the UK given that its finance was by then linked explicitly to the delivery of UK norms.

369 This is a salutary lesson for Wales. For 1993-94 the Welsh Office estimate that tax revenues of £9.3bn were raised in Wales against total Government expenditure of £14.7bn. Wales could not maintain existing levels of spending if it relied on its own tax revenues alone. But that does not detract from the principle of Wales being responsible for raising its own revenue as much as possible. The Liberal Democrats have said, for example, that those responsible for spending public money should also be responsible for raising it; and propose that the Senedd should have the power to raise or lower the rate of income tax by up to 3%.

370 There are two ways in which a Welsh Assembly could be financially more self-reliant; through assignment or sharing of taxes raised by central government; or through raising revenue directly itself. Tax assignment or revenue sharing would give the Welsh Government and the Welsh people a greater sense of entitlement to revenues raised in Wales, and would reduce the significance of the block grant; but there would still need to be a substantial block funding element, amounting to 50% of the Welsh block. Although Wales might call the assigned revenues her own, central government could offset changes in the assigned revenues through corresponding adjustments to the block, leaving the total revenue to Wales unchanged. Ultimate responsibility for setting the rates of tax would remain at the centre; and any changes at the margin (which each year is what counts) would continue to be made by the centre. Tax assignment would not give Wales the autonomy that would come from having a tax source under her own control.

371 The importance of having some revenues of her own was brought out in the recent study by the Institute for Fiscal Studies, *Financing Regional Government in Britain* (March 1996). That study drew an important distinction between decentralisation of **administration** and decentralisation of **choice**. If the principal purpose behind devolution to Wales is the more efficient implementation and administration of policies determined by central government, then it may be appropriate for the Welsh Government to be financed largely or entirely through central government transfers. But if the Welsh Government is to have genuine responsibility for making choices about the level and nature of public spending in Wales, rather than simply administering public spending decisions reached by central government, it would need some source of tax revenues under its own control. This would promote both independence and accountability in the Welsh Government's spending decisions.

372 In practice few regional governments in Europe have significant sources of revenue under their own control. The proportions vary from 50% for regional government in France to 2% in Spain. But they all have some revenue raising power of their own; and even if they choose not to

exercise it, this freedom at the margin is crucial to maintaining policy autonomy and local accountability. It would also help to reduce an obvious point of friction with central government, and with local government. Without it, central government would be the permanent scapegoat for all Wales' budgetary difficulties; and the only source of budgetary flexibility would be to precept upon the tax base of local authorities.

373 The Welsh Government could manage with only a limited regional tax covering a small proportion of its total spending, so long as at the margin it had scope to change its level of revenue. Local government shows the merits but also the limitations of this form of 'marginal accountability'. If the Welsh Government chose to spend more, this should result in an increase, pound for pound in the level of Welsh taxation. Extra spending should result in extra tax. However, where regional taxation contributed only a small proportion of the total Welsh budget there would be the familiar problems of high gearing, with small percentage changes in Welsh spending leading to much larger percentage changes in Welsh tax rates. The increase might be pound for pound, but if regional taxation contributed only 10% of the Welsh budget a 1% increase in expenditure would require a 10% increase in Welsh taxes. It also leaves scope for considerable central government influence so long as central government provides most of the budget.

374 There is no way round this dilemma. Excluding tax assignment, the broad options for the Welsh Government are:
- to be 100% dependent on block funding.
- to be largely dependent on block funding with limited revenue raising powers.
- to be largely self financing through its own tax revenues.

In theory the ideal solution is the third, but most countries have found it impossible to achieve in practice because central government has taken all the best taxes, and many of them are better collected centrally. The IFS study suggests that variable regional income tax would yield the biggest feasible revenue for devolved and regional governments. There is not space here to go into the merits; the main rival candidates were regional sales tax and regional assignment of non-domestic rates.

375 The difficulty is the sharp conflict between the theory and the practical realities. Without some revenue raising power the Assembly would be the only elected body in the country with full political accountability but zero fiscal accountability. Even local authorities have power to raise their own revenue, and to borrow; and below them community councils have the power to precept. But it may be difficult to establish a degree of fiscal independence at the start, if there is still some doubt about the role and powers of an Assembly in Wales. It may be that revenue raising power is something to be conferred later, or conferred at the start but only exercisable later: when the Assembly has become established and built up some credit locally, and when the need for some power to vary spending at the margin might have been demonstrated in practice.

Borrowing Powers and Limits

376 The Wales Act 1978 mirrored the system for the UK as a whole for establishing a Welsh consolidated fund and a Welsh loans fund. The former included all grant revenue, the latter a float up to £250m from which the Welsh Assembly could borrow (effectively from the UK Government) in order to meet shortfalls in the consolidated fund. In addition, the Welsh Executive could borrow up to £35m to cover short-term difficulties. The Act provided for a

Treasury guarantee of sums borrowed by the Assembly; and for the Assembly to endeavour to see that capital expenditure financed by borrowing remained within limits determined by the Secretary of State.

377 Similar arrangements will be required again to cover temporary shortfalls in grant revenue. Local government will retain its existing borrowing powers, but responsibility for monitoring such borrowing should be transferred to the Welsh Executive; and credit approval for individual loans would fall to the Welsh Executive. The UK Government may still need to retain some control on total borrowing partly for the 1970s reason, to help maintain overall control of the macro economy; and partly to meet the targets set by Maastricht. The fiscal convergence criteria for monetary union set out in the Protocol on the Excessive Deficit Procedure to the Maastricht Treaty - Government deficit no more than 3% of GDP, Government debt no more than 60% of GDP - suggest that, if anything, the desire for central control of borrowing may have increased. But many other EU member states allow regional governments to borrow without setting tight central limits - France and Germany for example. This requires different arrangements at the centre to keep track of borrowing commitments, and to forecast future developments in the national economy as a result. But it also acknowledges that the financial markets will impose their own discipline on regional governments; and that the interest on regional debt has to be found out of regional budgets.

Conclusion

378 This chapter has considered the different financing options at some length, because they are of crucial importance. Scotland and Wales enjoy relatively high levels of public expenditure, which would be likely to come under intense public and political scrutiny after devolution. The maintenance of the Barnett formula in its present form cannot be taken for granted. New machinery is required to underpin confidence in the financing system, and move towards a sustainable financial settlement which needs to satisfy the following criteria:

- it should be equitable and fair in terms of process between the nations and regions of the UK.
- it should respect the principle of equalisation and aim to match resources to needs between the different parts of the UK.
- it should be politically sustainable, providing reasonable financial stability for the Welsh Assembly even when relations between Cardiff and London are not good.
- it should operate within the financial constraints imposed on and from the centre e.g. Maastricht criteria, demands of macro economic policy.
- it should offer flexibility at the margin to cope with fluctuating revenue and unforeseen difficulties.
- it should be a transparent process with an independent Commission, responsible for guaranteeing the accuracy and objectivity of the data, auditing the application of the formula, and reviewing the formula itself as necessary - perhaps on the basis of a periodic needs assessment.
- it should promote a sense of fiscal responsibility and accountability.
- it should minimise the opportunities for conflict with local government and with central government.

378 Further, if a Welsh Assembly is to be financed by a formula-based allocation, as the Welsh Office is now, then the durability of that formula under the public and political scrutiny that devolution will entail cannot be guaranteed. If it did come under pressure, then an independent UK-wide needs assessment would be a necessary underpinning for a more stable and durable settlement for the future.

379 If the principal purpose behind devolution is the more efficient administration of policies determined by central government, then it is appropriate for the Welsh Government to continue to be funded entirely through block funding. But if the Welsh Government is to have responsibility for making real choices about the level and nature of public spending in Wales it will need power to raise some of its own revenue. The yield may not be significant, and it may create the gearing problems evident in the tax and spending decisions of local government; but without some revenue raising power the Welsh Assembly will have no fiscal accountability to the Welsh people. It may be a power to be conferred later, once the Assembly has become established.

Chapter 11

Electoral Systems and the Size of the Welsh Assembly

Introduction

381 It is generally accepted that there is no perfect electoral system. That is the view of most academic commentators; and it was the conclusion of the Plant Working Party on Electoral Systems established by the Labour Party in 1990. Each electoral system is a product of its own national and political context; and its effectiveness must be judged by a number of different criteria which are unlikely to prove compatible with each other.

382 The different criteria generally include considerations such as the extent to which a system promotes stable, effective and legitimate government; fairness of representation; a wide choice of representatives; and contact between the electorate and its chosen representatives. But there is disagreement on the relative priorities to be attached to each; and different systems strike the balance in different places. Nor is this an entirely abstract exercise; regard must be paid to a country's political development, geography and historical experience. Wales has relatively separate communities in the North and South, a division between English and Welsh speakers, and a history of political dominance by one party since the introduction of the franchise a hundred years ago (initially by the Liberals, and for most of this century by Labour). Any electoral system must take account of these factors, and must try to unite rather than divide the different communities in Wales.

383 In the absence of a forum such as the Scottish Constitutional Convention the opposition parties have not been able to agree on an electoral system for the Welsh Assembly. Plaid Cymru supports proportional representation using the additional member system (AMS), with 80 constituency members - half men, half women - and 20 additional members selected from a national list to give proportionality. The Liberal Democrats propose a Senedd to be elected by single transferable vote (STV) using multi-member constituencies, also producing a total of 100 members. The Parliament for Wales Campaign also supports STV.

384 The Wales Labour Party has come down in favour of 'first past the post', but during its consultation exercise considered a version of the additional member system which has been proposed by the Scottish Constitutional Convention for a Scottish Parliament. *Shaping the Vision* (May 1995) records: "It was in the area of the preferred method of election to the Assembly that there was most division of opinion amongst those who responded to the consultation. Views were evenly split between those who favoured the retention of the existing first past the post method of election and those who opted for a system which would reflect more accurately the proportion of votes cast".

The Choice of Electoral Systems

385 It is therefore necessary to consider how each system might be implemented, starting with a brief description of the differences between the systems. Put at its simplest, majoritarian systems are more concerned with producing strong government whereas proportional representation is more concerned with producing a representative parliament.

First Past The Post

386 This is the system used for electing the House of Commons, more properly known as the single-member plurality system. The candidate winning the largest number of votes in each constituency wins, whether or not the candidate has an overall majority. The system produces exaggerated majorities, translating a small plurality of the popular vote into a safe, working majority for the winning party. It secures disproportionate representation, which is held by defenders of the system to be an advantage since it increases the likelihood of a single party Government with a majority in the House of Commons, producing strong and effective government.

Single Transferable Vote

387 STV is used for European and local elections in Northern Ireland. It produces a high level of proportionality between votes cast and seats won; and thus secures fair representation for minority parties. This is achieved through transforming constituencies into fewer and larger geographical units, each of which elects a group of several MPs (normally four or five) instead of the present single member arrangement. Each party fields up to as many candidates as there are MPs to be elected, and voters indicate their preference by marking the ballot paper 1, 2, 3, etc. The count involves successive candidates achieving a set quota of votes, above which number second or next preferences are cast among the other candidates. It thus does away with wasted votes; votes which cannot be used for the election of a first choice candidate - either because they are not needed, or because he or she has no chance of victory - are transferred to another candidate who is able to use the vote. STV is occasionally criticised as too complex for voters to understand, but it operates perfectly well in trades union and private elections in the UK, and in certain other countries, with a very low proportion of invalid votes.

Additional Member System

388 The additional member system aims to combine the advantages of single member constituencies and proportionality. It would retain 'first past the post' elections for electing the constituency Members of the Assembly, with additional members being elected from national or regional lists of party candidates. This is the system used in Germany, where voters enter two crosses on the ballot paper: first for the candidate whom they support as their constituency MP, and second for their preferred political party. The object of the additional members is to compensate for such disproportionality as occurs from the constituency 'first past the post' election.

Outcomes under Different Electoral Systems

389 It is inevitably speculative to try and assess the likely outcome of any election under new rules and conditions. The voters will be faced with new choices and new means of expressing their preferences, leading to changes in voting behaviour. Nevertheless after the last general election in 1992, some interesting work was done by the Public Policy Group at the LSE on 'replaying' the 1992 election under different electoral systems. The table below extracts from their work the figures for Wales, showing the possible outcomes of different electoral systems by replaying the 1992 results[52]. The first column gives the percentage of the popular vote received by each of the major parties in 1992, and subsequent columns show the number and percentage of the 38 Welsh seats likely to have been received under the different systems.

Table 11   General Election in Wales Replayed

Proportion of Vote	NUMBER AND PROPORTION OF SEATS		
	First Past The Post (Actual result)	STV	AMS
Labour 50%	27 71%	18 47%	19 50%
Conservatives 29%	6 16%	9 24%	11 29%
Liberal Democrats 12%	1 3%	7 18%	5 13%
Plaid Cymru 10%	4 11%	4 11%	3 8%

Note: Percentages are rounded

390   The main difference in the figures above is between 'first past the post' and the two proportional systems; 'first past the post' yields a highly disproportionate result. Even with proportional representation, Labour is much the biggest single party, as it would have been in previous elections replayed under proportional representation systems. If proportional representation delivered these figures for a Welsh Assembly, the Labour Party could probably form a Government on its own.

Which System for Wales?

391   As already seen, although there is a multiplicity of possible electoral systems, in the policy discussions of the opposition parties there seem to be only three serious contenders: 'first past the post'; STV; and AMS.

392   As a backdrop to consideration of electoral systems for a Welsh Assembly, it is worth recording the thinking of the Scottish Constitutional Convention on alternative electoral systems for a Scottish Parliament. In devising an alternative electoral system, the Scottish Constitutional Convention laid down a number of criteria:
   - that it produces results in which the number of seats for various parties is broadly related to the number of votes cast for them.
   - that it ensures, or at least takes effective positive action to bring about, equal representation of men and women, and encourages fair representation of ethnic and other minority groups.
   - that it preserves a link between the member and his/her constituency.
   - that it is as simple as possible to understand.
   - that it ensures adequate representation of less populous areas.
   - that the system is designed to place the greatest possible power in the hands of the electorate.[53]

393 The Convention recognised the intrinsic difficulties in reconciling these six principles, some of which point towards a system of STV and others towards AMS. They came down in favour of AMS in the interests of speed, simplicity and comprehensibility. It would combine a familiar constituency element, and existing constituency boundaries - Westminster and European - could initially be used. The Convention recommended the election of 73 constituency members, elected by first past the post; and 56 additional members, elected from regional lists based on Scotland's eight Euro-constituencies (five additional members from each). The additional members should be allocated correctively, to compensate for the imbalances created in the 'first past the post' section. The party lists should be ordered by the parties themselves. They might contain the names of candidates also standing for election as constituency members, on the understanding that those elected to individual constituency seats would simply be replaced by the next name on the list (as happens in Germany).

First Past The Post

394 The existing system was chosen by the Labour Government in 1974, which decided that the new Scottish and Welsh Assemblies should be elected by 'first past the post'. The Government proposed to use the existing parliamentary constituencies in Scotland and Wales, each of which would return two members to the Assemblies. This was against a unanimous recommendation of the Royal Commission on the Constitution that any devolved Assemblies should be elected by STV:

> "An overriding requirement for the regional assemblies would be to ensure the proper representation of minorities....This would be particularly desirable in any region in which there were likely to be long periods without alternation of parties in power. We therefore favour the single transferable vote."[54]

395 During the long passage of the two devolution Bills various amendments to secure elections by proportional representation were presented but rejected in the Commons, although the Lords twice reinserted provision for proportional representation. In the Welsh referendum, the rejection of devolution was so massive that it cannot be argued that the question of the voting system affected the issue; but in Scotland it has been argued that the Labour Government's rejection of prortional representation was an important contributory factor in the defeat of its devolution proposals.[55]

Table 12 A Welsh Assembly Elected by First Past The Post

The 'first past the post' system could produce an Assembly of 80 members quite simply by using:
- existing Westminster constituencies (40 at the next general election).
- two candidates elected per constituency, electing both the first and the second past the post.

---

396 The main justification advanced for 'first past the post' is that it produces strong government, and that it is more effective at enabling the electorate to hold the Government accountable. By strong government, supporters of 'first past the post' mean single party Government. The exaggerated quality of the system ensures that any loss of votes by the Government is exaggerated in terms of seats, so that it does not take many votes to change hands for the Government to fall: and with single party Government it is obvious who should be punished for Government mistakes. But this presupposes a competitive two-party system. Where, as in Wales, one party is dominant, it is not necessary to have a 'first past the post' system to ensure single party Government; and so long as one party remains dominant, 'first past the post' makes it less likely that the Government will lose office.

397   The voting figures for Wales in the table from the 1992 general election show how strongly weighted is the result delivered by the 'first past the post 'system. Similar distortions in Scotland have led the Scottish Constitutional Convention to reject the first past the post system for electing a Scottish Parliament:

> "Confidence in the present electoral system has been badly undermined by the bitter experience of recent years. Elections in which the winner takes all become more difficult to defend... It is perfectly possible for a Member of Parliament to be returned with little more than one-third of the votes cast. The cumulative result can be the election of a Government with a substantial majority in Parliament but a minority share of the votes... The issue gave rise to considerable discussion in the Convention. The problems of fragmentation and the tendency to coalition government were canvassed, but the decisive factor was the need for a system under which the seats won more accurately reflected the votes cast for each party. It was for this reason that the Convention decided that the first-past-the-post system would not be used in electing the Scottish Parliament."[56]

398   Prior to the Scottish Constitutional Convention's final report, the Labour Party's working party on electoral systems - chaired by Lord Plant - also came down in favour of AMS for the Scottish Parliament (this recommendation was subsequently approved by the National Executive Committee of the Labour Party). No recommendation was made by the working party on an electoral system for Wales. Lord Plant has since explained their reasoning as follows

> "The Scottish Parliament had to be made acceptable to the Scottish people as a whole and this made it important that the electoral system for a Scottish Parliament should be of a sort to allow for a degree of pluralism in its representation and not to create what might for many years be seen as a one party state. A degree of proportionality was therefore seen by the party to be necessary to create an overall sense of legitimacy for the Scottish Parliament."

399   He went on to highlight the links between the Scottish and Welsh proposals:

> "It is interesting to compare this position with political opinion in Wales over the electoral system for the Welsh assembly. As I have said, the Working Party was suspended before it was able to make recommendations about the Welsh assembly, so the deliberations of the party in Wales were not informed by a recommendation from the Working Party or the NEC. In fact the Welsh conference has decided that the Welsh assembly should be elected by first past the post. This decision has been met with exactly the reaction from its opponents that the Scottish proposals avoided. Critics of the Welsh proposals, particularly the Liberal Democrats who favour a Welsh assembly, argue that this decision will turn the Welsh assembly into a one party body for the foreseeable future."[57]

Single Transferable Vote

400   The Liberal Democrats support STV as their preferred system for electing a Welsh Assembly. It is the system which has long been supported by the Electoral Reform Society; and when the UK has experimented with PR, STV has been the system of choice. STV was the voting system introduced to elect the new Northern Irish Parliament in 1922, and the Irish Dail. More recently STV was chosen for the Northern Ireland Assembly (in 1973 and 1982) and the Convention (1975) and it is used for Euro elections and local government elections in Northern Ireland. Although the elections to the Forum in May 1996 adopted a combination of national and constituency lists, that was a one-off which is unlikely to be repeated: any future Assembly in Northern Ireland seems likely to be elected by STV.

401 The main advantages claimed for STV are:
- it offers a high degree of proportionality (so long as the constituencies are large enough).
- it emphasises fairness to voters not to parties.
- it enables voters to discriminate between candidates of the same party, fine tuning their representation and maintaining tight accountability between voters and their representatives.
- it gives a better chance to independent candidates (important in rural Wales), who under AMS might be excluded from party lists.

402 **Table 13** sets out a scheme showing how a Welsh Assembly might be elected by STV based upon 20 multi-member constituencies.[58] Each constituency would be formed by pairing two of the 40 Westminster constituencies that will exist at the next general election, so that there would not be need for any boundary changes. The table shows the constituencies, their electorates, and the number of Members elected for each constituency. The total number of Members would be either 110 or 90 depending on whether the median ratio of electors to members is 20,000 to 1 or 25,000 to 1. For a 90 member Assembly constituencies would return either 4 or 5 members (depending on size); for an Assembly of 110 members each constituency would return either 5 or 6 members. The figures are illustrative, and the number does not always reflect the median ratio: in particular, each constituency has been given a minimum of five seats in the 110-member scheme; and a minimum of four seats in the 90-member scheme. The 110 member scheme is preferable purely from a proportionality point of view.

Additional Member System

403 The main advantages claimed for AMS are:
- AMS is likely to be the system chosen for a Scottish Parliament; this might be seen as a closer parallel than any Assembly in Northern Ireland.
- AMS retains single member constituencies.
- AMS is less threatening for political parties.

Two other arguments should be mentioned only to be dismissed:
- By using existing Westminster boundaries AMS could be speedily introduced (as we have seen so could STV).
- Pressures from Europe may point towards the use of regional list systems. Europe is committed to harmonising the different national electoral systems used for electing the European Parliament. STV is unknown in Europe, where most forms of PR are based upon regional or national party lists. But the de Gucht report on electoral systems for the European Parliament (which has been approved by the European Parliament) has suggested that any proportional representation scheme would suffice, including STV in regional constituencies as practised in Ireland.

The main disadvantage is regarded as the power given to the political parties in drawing up the party lists.

Table 13 STV Elections to a Welsh Assembly

Paired Westminster Constituencies	Electorates	Combined Electorates	Number of Members per Constituency	
			Ratio of 1 per:	
			20,000	(25,000)
Alyn & Deeside Delyn	57815 54713	112528	6	(5)
Clwyd South Wrexham	53963 51318	105281	5	(4)
Clwyd West Vale of Clwyd	53827 53013	106840	5	(4)
Conwy Ynys Mon	54469 54149	108618	5	(4)
Caernarfon Meirionnydd Nant Conwy	47095 32866	79961	5	(4)
Brecon & Radnorshire Montgomeryshire	52488 42137	94625	5	(4)
Ceredigion Preseli Pembrokeshire	54467 54295	108762	5	(4)
Carmarthen E & Dinefwr Carmarthen W & S Pem.	53256 55393	108649	5	(4)
Gower Llanelli	58389 59729	118118	6	(5)
Aberavon Neath	52038 56903	108941	5	(4)
Swansea East Swansea West	59421 60098	119519	6	(5)
Merthyr Tyd & Rhymney Caerphilly	58939 64995	123934	6	(5)
Cynon Valley Pontypridd	50026 63545	113571	6	(5)
Rhondda Ogmore	60467 53322	113789	6	(5)
Bridgend Vale of Glamorgan	59434 67152	126586	6	(5)
Cardiff Central Cardiff S & Penarth	58724 62216	120940	6	(5)
Cardiff North Cardiff West	57223 59470	116693	6	(5)
Newport East Newport West	51577 55294	106871	5	(4)
Blaenau Gwent Islwyn	56170 51927	108097	5	(4)
Monmouth Torfaen	59908 61726	121634	6	(5)
Total Welsh Electorate **Total Members**	**2,223,957**	**2,223,957**	110	(90)

Note: Electorate figures as at 9 November 1993.

404 There are a number of factors to be considered in developing an electoral system based on AMS; these are examined below. Table 14 suggests how a Welsh Assembly might be elected by the additional member system.

Table 14 A Welsh Assembly Elected by AMS

Using the additional member system to create an Assembly of 80 members could involve:
- 40 members elected by first past the post in single member Westminster constituencies.
- 40 additional members elected from regional party lists, based on Wales' five Euro-constituencies, with 8 additional members per constituency.

Size of the Assembly

405 The additional member system best ensures proportionality when there are equal numbers of constituency and party list MPs. In Germany the ratio is 50:50. But in Scotland the Constitutional Convention, taking Scotland's 72 Westminster constituencies as the basis for the constituency members, felt that a parliament of 144 would be too large. It has proposed 56 additional members, producing a parliament of 129 and a ratio of 57:43 between constituency and additional members.

406 Wales will have 40 Westminster constituencies at the next general election. Following the Scottish precedent the number of additional members could be limited to 20 or 30, but the difference between a total Assembly of 60 or 80 members does not seem significant. It would be better to start with a properly functioning proportional system. This suggests an Assembly of 80 members, 40 elected by first past the post in single member constituencies and 40 additional members elected from party lists.

Regional or National Lists

407 Should there be a single party list for the whole of Wales, or regional party lists? To retain a broad geographical spread and a link between additional members and constituencies it would seem desirable for there to be regional lists. The Scottish proposals might be adopted of basing regional lists on Wales' five Euro constituencies with eight additional members per constituency.

Who Orders the List?

408 Finally, should voters be allowed to alter the order of candidates as determined by the parties on their lists? This is a live question in Germany, where in Bavaria voters can use their second vote to alter the order. The Federal Committee of Enquiry into Constitutional Reform has recommended the general introduction of 'limited unordered lists' (limited in the sense that the voter is not able to add new names to the list). This might be a sensible refinement to incorporate in Wales, to avoid the concerns reported in Germany that the list system has led to excessive domination by the political parties. In an article in *Die Zeit* on 19 June 1992 President Von Weizsäcker bemoaned "that in Germany political recruitment is exclusively the concern of the parties. They are virtually alone in deciding who is to be candidate for what office. The main feature of the professional politician in Germany consists of supporting what the party wants, so that it will nominate you - preferably high up on the list". He went on to refer specifically to the need of the electorate to have "greater influence on the choice of candidates on the list".[59]

Other Issues

409   Two remaining details should be mentioned. First is whether there should be a 5% threshold, as in Germany, which excludes parties attracting a very small minority vote. There should be no need for such a provision in Wales, because with only 40 seats allocated amongst five Euro constituencies parties standing for additional member seats will have to reach a threshold of at least 5% of the party-preference vote, in that Euro-constituency, to have a chance of entering the Assembly.

410   Second is the concern sometimes expressed in the UK about AMS that it creates two classes of MPs.[60] However, this is not the experience in Germany. One of the leading experts on the German system, Professor Eckhard Jesse, has written

> "There is absolutely no difference in the way constituency members and list members go about their business. List members, too, nurse their constituencies, since the great majority of them are also candidates at constituency level. It is not true to say that there are 'two types of MPs'. In practice the nomination procedure is such that parties ensure that their constituency candidates have a safety net in the form of a safe place on the list. A promising candidate will be elected either by the constituency or via the list. Most women members are elected via the lists".[61]

However some say that special factors have made the list more acceptable in Germany than it might be here, where list members might come to be regarded as second class.[62]

Dual Membership and Co-option

411   The Wales Act 1978 would have disqualified MPs (but not Peers) from sitting in the Welsh Assembly. There is bound to be concern at the quality of candidates for election to a Welsh Assembly, and it seems unfortunate to exclude national politicians at the outset by forcing them to resign from the House of Commons. When the European Parliament held its first elections there was no bar on MPs standing, and this remains the case. With the demanding workload in both Parliaments the situation has gradually found its own level, and only two MPs are now also MEPs. So with the Welsh Assembly there should be no restriction, at least for its first term, while MPs decide whether they want to be members of the Assembly or to continue to sit at Westminster. We noted in chapter 6 that membership of the Assembly need not be a full-time occupation. Some overlapping membership is desirable to help reduce conflict between the two legislatures, but few members will want to continue sitting in both and the electorate may punish them if they do. In the longer term, overlapping membership might best be achieved through selected members of the Welsh Assembly sitting in a reformed House of Lords, as discussed in Chapter 12.

412   The other source of experienced politicians is members of local authorities. Here too it seems desirable to encourage overlapping membership, to ensure that the Assembly has understanding and respect for local authorities as equal partners in the business of government. The responsibilities of a councillor are less demanding than those of an MP and there need be no long term conflict between the two roles. (In some European legislatures such links are encouraged, but not at Westminster). Informal links of this kind will not obviate the need for more formal liaison machinery with local government, and some committees of the Assembly may want to co-opt local authority members as recommended in Chapter 9.

Conclusion

413 The choice lies between a majoritarian system (such as 'first past the post') or a system of proportional representation. Majoritarian systems are more concerned with producing strong government, and PR with producing a representative parliament. A proportional representation system is likely to be adopted in both Northern Ireland and Scotland. It has been proposed in Wales, to offer a sense of involvement to the minority parties and to quell fears that the Assembly will be dominated by the Labour Party and by the interests of South Wales; a degree of proportionality may also be necessary to create an overall sense of legitimacy.

414 Two forms of proportional representation could be considered. For certain elections in Northern Ireland they use the single transferable vote; for a Scottish Parliament it has been proposed to use the German additional member system. Either system could be adapted for use in Wales to produce an Assembly of around 80-100 members.

415 Different features of the two systems are:
STV
- emphasises fairness to voters not to parties.
- enables voters to discriminate between candidates of the same party.
- gives a better chance to independent candidates.
- requires multi-member constituencies.

AMS
- retains single member constituencies.
- follows the analogy with Scotland.
- gives power to the political parties in drawing up the party lists.

416 The Assembly is unlikely to sit more than 100 days a year, so that membership of the Welsh Assembly may not be a full-time occupation. There should be no restriction on MPs and local government councillors standing for election. Thereafter dual membership can be left to find its own level determined by the workload and views of constituents.

Chapter 12

Entrenchment and Resolution of Disputes

Introduction

417 In Scotland the Constitutional Convention has devoted considerable ingenuity trying to devise ways to entrench the new settlement so that Westminster cannot revoke it or curtail the powers of a new Scottish Parliament. Are similar safeguards required in Wales to protect the Welsh Assembly? The first part of this chapter considers the feasibility of *legal* safeguards, and the second and third parts consider different *political* solutions to the question of entrenchment. The remainder of the chapter then considers the resolution of disputes: when disputes might arise, how the Government and other parties might challenge acts of the Welsh Assembly, and which court should be the final arbiter of such disputes.

Legal Entrenchment

418 It is not easy within the Westminster tradition of parliamentary sovereignty to find ways of restricting that sovereignty, even by self-denying ordinance. In countries with written constitutions it is quite common for the constitution to provide special safeguards (referendum, two-thirds majority in parliament, etc.) making it more difficult to change fundamentals of the constitution. In particular in federal systems it is generally impossible for the central government to alter the powers and privileges of the states or provinces without their consent. Both central and state governments operate under the constitution in a manner unknown in the UK. The UK Parliament can do or undo anything it likes, including abolishing other tiers of government: as was seen with the abolition of the Stormont Parliament in Northern Ireland in 1972.

419 The same dependent status will await a Welsh Assembly: 'power devolved is power retained'. Whatever restraints Westminster might build into the devolution settlement, it can subsequently override or ignore, so long as a majority at Westminster wills it. In one respect this flexibility is a good thing: it is undesirable for any constitutional settlement to be set in stone, and changing political, economic and social developments may require the arrangements for any Welsh Assembly to be changed, perhaps fundamentally, in ways which cannot now be foreseen. The Act of Union 1707 had to be amended several times within a century of its signature;[63] and the pace of change has grown enormously since the eighteenth century. The Welsh settlement will certainly need amending from time to time. Should safeguards be built in to try to ensure that it is not amended against the wishes of the people of Wales?

420 Ideally the devolution settlement should not be capable of being amended unilaterally. It is not possible completely to fetter the discretion of a future Parliament; but a number of ways have been suggested of making it more difficult for Parliament to overturn the Welsh Assembly.

421 The first is that the legislation establishing the Welsh Assembly could provide that no bill to alter its powers could be presented to Parliament without the consent of the Welsh Assembly. This could not prevent Parliament from subsequently removing the requirement; but it would place a strong impediment in the way of a UK Government seeking to amend the powers of the Welsh Assembly unilaterally.

422 The Scottish Constitutional Convention has proposed that, instead of placing entrenchment provisions in a bill to establish a Scottish Parliament, the UK Parliament should be invited to make a solemn declaration in advance of considering the legislation that the Act founding the

Scottish Parliament should not be repealed without the consent of the Scottish Parliament and of the Scottish people directly consulted through general election or referendum.[64] The Convention feared that the controversial nature of entrenchment provisions, and the challenge they pose to parliamentary sovereignty, might delay the passage of devolution legislation. A declaration is not as strong a form of entrenchment, and entrenchment in the Bill is preferable. If a Welsh devolution bill followed in a separate parliamentary session from a Scottish devolution bill (as discussed in the next chapter), it would suffice to see what degree of entrenchment the Scots had succeeded in establishing.

423   The final possibility is the inclusion of a 'notwithstanding clause' in the legislation establishing a Welsh Assembly. The clause would provide that if a subsequent Act is inconsistent with key provisions of the Welsh Assembly Act, then the subsequent Act should be ineffective unless it contains express provision that it is to take effect notwithstanding its incompatibility with the Welsh Assembly Act. Such a clause is generally proposed as a means of entrenching a Bill of Rights, which might otherwise have no institutional guardian. In the case of Wales it seems unnecessary: the Assembly should be the primary guardian of its powers and future.

Referendum

424   If legal entrenchment is impossible, what other forms of entrenchment might help to protect the new Welsh Assembly against abolition following a change of Government, or a cooling in relations between Westminster and Cardiff? It is helpful to distinguish between a referendum as a means of entrenchment, to guard against the *abolition* of the Assembly; and the referendum as a consultative or legitimating device, linked to the *creation* of the Assembly. The latter is considered further below.

425   The former is essentially another form of legal entrenchment. The devolution legislation could provide that the Welsh Assembly could not be abolished without first holding a referendum to seek the views of the people of Wales. It would be disproportionate to require a referendum for every change to the powers of the Assembly (some of which will be minor and technical); but outright abolition is a much bigger step. The referendum requirement could also be circumvented subsequently; but again it would place a political obstacle in the way of an abolitionist UK Government.

426   Abolition cannot be regarded as a purely hypothetical risk following the demise of the metropolitan counties and the GLC in the mid-1980s. It will take the Assembly a while to become an effective body which earns its place under the sun through its achievements. Its birth will give rise to painful transitions for all associated agencies; additional costs must be incurred before any offsetting savings can accrue; and it will be during the infancy of the Assembly that it may be particularly vulnerable.

427   The vulnerability of the Assembly may be increased if it is created in circumstances of highly charged political controversy, amid accusations that it is not wanted by the people of Wales. One way of testing whether it is wanted is by holding a referendum. Demands for a referendum are generally associated with opponents of a Welsh Assembly; but a referendum could be used by a Government which supports the establishment of an Assembly, as a means of advancing its

policy. It might also serve as a political form of entrenchment, as it would be more difficult for a different Government to abolish the Assembly if the people of Wales had shown that they supported its creation.

428   There is no constitutional doctrine which says that a referendum is required in these circumstances. The political parties maintain that a referendum is unnecessary: the people of Wales will have spoken at the next general election, when three out of the four parties in Wales will campaign for an Assembly. To this others reply that general elections are rarely held on a single issue: people vote on all the items in the political parties' manifestos and on their impressions of the competence of the rival political parties in managing the economy, defence, raising or lowering taxes, etc.

Lessons from the 1979 Referendum

429   The Labour Government in the 1970s also maintained that a referendum was unnecessary. It was conceded in response to parliamentary pressure during the first Scotland and Wales Bill; and in March 1979 the people of Wales rejected the assembly proposed in the Wales Act 1978 by four to one. What lessons can be learnt from that experience?

430   The first lesson is that however stout the Government's position there will be considerable pressure to hold a referendum. The precedent of the 1970s will be cited; as will the promised referendum in Northern Ireland, and the regional referendums which the Labour Party is proposing before introducing regional assemblies in England.[65] There will almost certainly be a challenge by judicial review to force a referendum, as was attempted in relation to the Maastricht Treaty. It is unlikely to succeed; but it will add to the pressure. If the political pressure proves hard to resist, then a Government might consider offering a referendum from the outset rather than conceding one once it has run into difficulties. And if a referendum is offered up front, it is worth considering whether it might best be held in advance of the legislation or after its parliamentary passage.

431   This is the second lesson from the 1970s: whether a referendum is best held before or after introduction of the legislation. There are arguments both ways. In Northern Ireland, the current Government is proposing that a referendum be held before any legislation to recreate a devolved Parliament, as part of the 'triple lock' to ensure that any new arrangements in the province are based upon widespread consent. If the Welsh referendum had been held in 1974 a great deal of parliamentary time might have been saved and subsequent grief avoided. As we saw in chapter 2, the knowledge that a referendum was to be held had a deleterious effect on the parliamentary debates in the 1970s. The committee stage became a long drawn out second reading debate in which MPs continued to challenge the principle of the Bill; and many of the amendments tabled were put down not to improve the Bill, but as markers for the subsequent referendum campaign.

432   The arguments for holding a referendum after the legislation are that the people of Wales need a specific proposition to vote upon. An Act of Parliament is more specific than a statement of the Government's intentions in a White Paper whose proposals may subsequently be altered. There is also the practical difficulty that holding a referendum itself requires legislation: if held in advance there would need to be a separate enabling bill for the referendum, which otherwise could be authorised in the main legislation.

433 Finally there are technical questions about the status of the referendum, the framing of the question, the required majority, and the way votes are counted. Within our system of parliamentary sovereignty the referendum can only be advisory; it cannot decide an issue. That is for Parliament; but Parliament would naturally pay close attention to a referendum result. It is unlikely that the Wales Act 1978 would have been implemented had the Labour Government been re-elected in 1979.

434 The referendum question is normally framed by the Government of the day and approved by Parliament in the legislation authorising the referendum. In 1979 there was a straight 'Yes' and 'No' vote and the votes were counted across the eight counties of Wales. It has been suggested that a future referendum might be consultative about key aspects of the Assembly; that it could ask whether the Assembly should have legislative or revenue raising power, and how it should be elected. In practice it is extremely difficult to devise a satisfactory 'preferendum' on these lines. A referendum works better when there is a specific proposition which the voters are invited to endorse or reject.

435 The technical issues posed by referendums are being addressed by the Commission on the Conduct of Referendums, whose report will be published by the Constitution Unit later in 1996.

National and Regional Representation at Westminster

436 The second form of political entrenchment is to strengthen Welsh representation at Westminster. In federal systems the position of the states is buttressed not simply by defining their powers in the constitution but by having representation of the states in the federal legislature. There can be no question of increasing the number of Welsh MPs in the House of Commons; if anything the reverse (see chapter 7). By analogy with federal systems, it is in the upper house that one would look to strengthen the representation of the nations and regions.

437 A reformed House of Lords could play a significant role in knitting together a post-devolution settlement by representing at the centre the interests of the regions. The Constitution Unit's earlier report, *Reform of the House of Lords,* set out a number of possible models for an elected second chamber. There are two ways in which the regions might be represented: through the direct election of individuals (as in the American and Australian Senate), or through nominating representatives of the regional governments, as in the German Bundesrat. It is in this chamber that the balance of power is continuously re-adjusted between the German government and the Länder, the distribution of the budget is negotiated, and deals are struck between political leaders. It is a highly functional part of the German federal system and a model worth considering for the UK.

438 Reforms at Westminster may in the long run be as important as the design of a Welsh Assembly in forming a balanced and long lasting devolution package; and a reformed second chamber could play a significant part both in protecting the interests of the regions and in helping to maintain the Union.

Resolution of Disputes

When Disputes Might Arise

439 Whenever political institutions are created there are bound to be uncertainties and disagreements about the extent of their powers, which ultimately have to be resolved in the courts. This a fact of life in any democratic state which observes the rule of law. In the UK, all public bodies - the Welsh Office, local authorities, quangos - are subject to the rule of law, and can be challenged if they exceed or abuse their powers. The *right* of challenge through the courts is an important freedom, which must be preserved in any devolution legislation; but the legislation must be designed so that the *likelihood* of challenge is kept to a minimum.

440 Ways of minimising recourse to the courts and resolving disputes by conciliation or negotiation were discussed at the end of chapter 5. The legislation needs to be designed with built-in flexibility and with structures to emphasise the need for co-operation and the political resolution of disputes wherever possible. But however well the legislation is drafted and however successful the procedure for resolving disputes by negotiation, disputes will arise as to whether the Assembly or the Executive has exceeded its powers which call for a legal ruling. (Unless some effective form of entrenchment is created, legal questions as to Parliament exceeding its powers cannot arise under devolution legislation).

441 Challenge to Welsh legislation might arise because the Welsh Assembly had strayed beyond its jurisdiction under its own parent Act, or because the legislation was said to be in breach of European or international law. In the next section of this chapter we consider the different circumstances in which disputes might arise, by taking in sequence the different stages at which Welsh legislation or acts of the Welsh Government might be challenged.

Pre-legislative Challenge

442 The earliest stage when a challenge might arise is when a bill is first introduced into the Asembly. This is too early a stage to allow reference to the courts. It is virtually unknown overseas to allow reference at such a stage; the dispute may be a political one, and not something into which the courts should be drawn when there is a political means of resolution at hand through amendment of the bill.

443 If the Assembly needs reassurance that the bill is *prima facie* within its jurisdiction, that can be done through a certificate from the Speaker, who can seek advice from the Clerk to the Assembly. The Northern Ireland Constitution Act 1973 required the Clerk to the Assembly to consider the matter both on introduction and again before completion of the legislative process. A similar procedure might be followed for the Welsh Assembly, leading to the ruling out of any provisions that the officers of the Assembly concluded were outside the Assembly's competence. Alternatively, this task could be performed by a standing committee of the Assembly.

Post-legislative Scrutiny: 1978 Provisions

444 Questions as to the competence of the Assembly to legislate on a particular matter can arise before the enactment of legislation is completed. The Scotland Act, section 19(1), required the Secretary of State to consider every bill passed by the Assembly and to refer to the Judicial Committee of the Privy Council for a decision on its *vires* if he was of the opinion that:

- any of its provisions were outwith the Assembly's competence; or
- there was sufficient doubt about it to justify the reference (in this case the reference was in the Secretary of State's discretion).

A bill containing a provision held to be *ultra vires* by the Judicial Committee could not be submitted for Assent.

445   These provisions were in addition to the powers of the Secretary of State:
- to prevent Assent if the bill was incompatible with Community or other obligations.
- to refer an Assembly bill to Parliament for disallowance on the grounds that it might affect a reserved matter and it was not in the public interest to enact it.

446   It was argued at the time that under this process, an Act of the Assembly would be law only to the extent that a provision had been adjudged to be *intra vires* and that the status of an Act that had not been considered by the Judicial Committee would remain uncertain. Accordingly it has been suggested that if a bill had not been referred to the Judicial Committee or if the Judicial Committee had not found it to be *ultra vires*, no further challenge should be permitted to the Act. Section 19(4) provided for the finality of any ruling by the Judicial Committee on the validity of any provision referred to it.

447   Few jurisdictions have adopted a procedure of this kind. It has serious weaknesses, as it assumes that all possible questions of *vires* can be identified in abstract by legal advisers in advance of the legislation being put into operation. It is often only when issues of fact arise that questions of validity of applicable legislation become evident. Circumstances and legal values change; and faced with a challenge once the legislation has started to bite, and a real set of facts, the courts may come to a different conclusion from a preliminary ruling given in the abstract.

Post-Enactment Reference

448   It is preferable for provision to be made for a possible reference to the courts once an Act has passed through all its legislative stages (including Royal Assent), and has become a law. In most federal systems there is provision for an immediate reference to the constitutional court for a ruling upon enactment. The likelihood of a challenge will have probably been flagged up during passage of the bill. Provision could be made for empowering the Law Officers of the Welsh and UK Governments to refer any issue of vires for a court ruling. This fast-track procedure can be expected to be instituted immediately after enactment, but some time limits may have to be placed upon the making of such general references.

449   This procedure might be restricted to the Law Officers (as in the Scotland Act, Schedule 12); alternatively other bodies or persons that are materially affected if the legislation is put in force might be recognised as having *locus standi* to institute such proceedings in their own names or by a relator action, for example a Welsh local authority or some other public body which might have expected to perform particular functions affected by the suspect legislation. In such a case, the Law Officers should be informed immediately and authorised to intervene in respect of the devolution issue.

450   The court should be authorised to make a declaration as to the *vires* of the provisions questioned and that decision should be made binding in all legal proceedings. It is unnecessary to give the court more coercive powers. This is not the practice with respect to other public law

proceedings against the Crown (of which the Assembly would be an emanation). The Assembly and the Executive can be expected to institute the appropriate steps to correct the position.

451   There is no reason why a similar procedure should not be similarly available *at any time* to challenge actions of the Welsh Executive as beyond its devolved competence or because the Executive was acting under legislation beyond the Assembly's competence. The question of remedies would be treated in the same way as cases for the judicial review of executive actions.

References in the Course of Legal Proceedings

452   Issues as to the validity of Assembly legislation or the competence of the Executive to take particular action may well arise in the normal course of litigation. Such matters could be settled by the court or tribunal concerned, and would have to be if the devolution legislation makes no other provision. Although consistency of approach may be secured through appeal mechanisms, certain issues are likely to be too complex for at least some of the courts or tribunals in which they arise. The Scotland Act (Schedule 12) provided a procedure permitting devolution issues to be referred to the next level in the court hierarchy with a final appeal to the Judicial Committee of the Privy Council. Devolution issues arising in the House of Lords as a rule were to be referred to the Judicial Committee.

453   Clearer provision might be made in the Welsh legislation analogous to that authorised by Article 177 of the Treaty of Rome for dealing with questions of European law, and now well established UK practice. This would permit a reference to be made by a court or tribunal in which a devolution issue arose to one court (for example the Judicial Committee) for an advisory opinion on the legal question of devolved competence. This ruling would be binding as to the interpretation of the point of law referred to the court, but it would be left to the referring court to reach its own judgement on the matter after applying that interpretation. The question of remedies and *locus standi* of parties to the litigation would be dealt with, following standard practice, according to the type of proceedings brought.

Which Court?

454   In principle, these issues might seem to warrant the creation of a new constitutional court with the function of dealing with all devolution matters. Such a step might be appropriate as part of a new constitutional settlement, but it is difficult to make a case for it merely to decide devolution issues concerning Wales and Scotland. The devolution legislation has no special legal status requiring special protection and does not give rise to major constitutional innovations that require the creation of a new court. Existing institutions are capable of dealing with the kinds of issues that can be anticipated.

455   That said, the role played by the court which is given the task of finally deciding devolution issues could make a significant impact on the devolution arrangements. Judicial construction of the legislation could be narrow and protective or expansive and creative; the results could materially affect the success of devolution. What is also clear is that the same court is likely to be designated both for the Welsh and the Scottish schemes and that the choice agreed for Scotland will be that applied to Wales.

456 The choice lies between the Appellate Committee of the House of Lords (which is the final court of appeal for England and Wales and Northern Ireland and for civil matters for Scotland) and the Judicial Committee of the Privy Council. In practice, the judges assigned to both are mostly the same persons although the composition of the Judicial Committee is both wider and larger. The House of Lords comprises the Lord Chancellor and 12 Lords of Appeal in Ordinary who may be supplemented by former Lord Chancellors, retired Lords of Appeal and any other peers who have held high judicial office in any part of the United Kingdom. By convention, two of the Law Lords are Scottish, but no special recognition is given to judges with Welsh or Northern Ireland connections. The Judicial Committee consists of persons appointed as Privy Councillors who hold or have held high judicial office in any part of the UK (and a number of senior judges from countries from which appeals still lie).

457 Some arguments that are said to favour the Judicial Committee are not especially convincing. For example, it is argued that the members of the Appellate Committee may be perceived as members of the very Parliament whose powers are being devolved or as predominantly English in their judicial backgrounds. This contrasts sharply with the fact that the Law Lords are thought to discharge the functions of the final court of appeal satisfactorily in other matters. Similarly, the fact that the Judicial Committee has, institutionally, developed case law from Canada and Australia on jurisdictional disputes arising from their constitutions carries little weight, given that those matters were decided by long past generations of judges, that the case law is available to the House of Lords and that the current Law Lords have extensive contemporary experience of constitutional interpretation as members of the Judicial Committee.

458 One argument favours assigning the functions of final court of appeal to the House of Lords. If issues arise in the House of Lords in the course of other proceedings, should that court be permitted to decide the matter or should it be required to refer the devolution issue to the Judicial Committee? The Scotland Act (Schedule 12) required that such a matter had to be referred to the Judicial Committee "unless the House considers it more appropriate, having regard to all the circumstances, that they should determine the issue". This is a recipe for disputes between the court which is, in most matters, the final court of the UK's various legal systems and a court which hitherto has been outside them and which performs no other appellate functions within them. Further, whilst a precedent of the Judicial Committee would presumably bind the House of Lords, the reverse would not be the case. Such an arrangement would introduce an element of friction and unpredictability at the very apex of the legal systems.

459 In principle, the Judicial Committee offers greater flexibility in providing a larger resource of judges which can be increased more easily perhaps than the Appellate Committee to include some with connections with Wales, Scotland and Northern Ireland. But whichever court is selected, it must be presumed that in Scottish cases, a court of five would be expected to include at least two judges with senior experience in the Scottish courts. It is by means clear that similar statutory guarantees could be provided for Wales, since no judge is appointed to hold office solely in courts in Wales. National origins or similar links constitute a different basis for selection, which should not be used for one jurisdiction only. Other problems may arise if it is felt that English, Welsh and Northern Irish judges should also be present in every matter because the activities of the court have implications for the UK at large. This could reduce the number of English judges to one in some cases, which may be politically unacceptable. One course of action then would be to increase the size of the court to seven.

460   In practice most devolution issues are likely to be decided by the House of Lords. Under the Government of Ireland Act 1920, although the Government had power to refer questions of *vires* arising from Northern Ireland legislation to the Judicial Committee for determination, almost all such matters were dealt with by the House of Lords on appeal in the course of ordinary litigation. This suggests that references by a Government under a fast track procedure should also be to the House of Lords. The jurisdiction of the Privy Council is declining to the point of near extinction; and the membership of the two panels is essentially the same. But it does point up that in the long run the only satisfactory solution may be the creation of a constitutional or supreme court, separate from the House of Lords and Parliament. These are issues to which the Constitution Unit intends to return in a later report.

Conclusion

461   Any division of powers ultimately depends upon legal interpretation in the courts. Devolution legislation must provide for an early test of the *vires* of legislation passed by the Welsh Assembly. Upon enactment the Law Officers and others affected should be able to refer the new legislation on a fast-track procedure to the courts. This could be to the Privy Council (as proposed in 1978) or the Appellate Committee of the House of Lords. To prevent uncertainty at the apex of the legal system it seems preferable for the final court of appeal on devolution issues to be the House of Lords.

462   It is impossible within the Westminster tradition of sovereignty to find satisfactory ways of entrenching the powers or the existence of the Welsh Assembly. More effective than legal entrenchment might be political entrenchment by a referendum. It would be more difficult for a future Government to abolish the Assembly if the people of Wales had shown they supported its creation. If a referendum is offered, it would be better to hold it in advance of the legislation (as proposed for Northern Ireland) rather than afterwards (as happened in 1978). But holding a referendum in advance would require enabling legislation to authorise expenditure on the referendum.

463   An institutional safeguard for the longer term would be to strengthen Welsh representation at Westminster, not in the House of Commons but in a reformed House of Lords, remodelled to represent the nations and regions of the UK.

Chapter 13

The Timetable and Costs of Implementation

The Need for Public Debate

464 It was noted in chapter 2 how the proposals for Scotland dominated the devolution debates in the 1970s. Even when there were two separate Bills, the Wales Bill followed so hard on the heels of the Scotland Bill that it remained in its shadow; and during the referendum campaign in 1979 Welsh voters received far more media coverage of Scottish than Welsh devolution. It would not be surprising if the Welsh electorate had only a confused and hazy idea of the proposals in the Wales Act 1978.

465 In the 1990s Wales risks being overshadowed by Scotland again. In Scotland there has been an intense debate instigated by the Scottish Constitutional Convention, which has published half a dozen reports and consultative documents since its inaugural meeting in 1989. The Convention has embraced the Scottish Labour and Liberal Democrat parties, Scottish MPs and MEPs, all Scotland's local authorities, the churches, trades unions and other interests. Its plans for Scotland's Parliament may not be the talk of the Glasgow pubs, but it has certainly engaged the attention of the political classes.

466 In Wales no such debate has taken place. The Parliament for Wales Campaign organised a Democracy Conference in Llandridod Wells in 1994, and published the conference papers in a book; and it has prepared a draft Bill. But there has been no pooling of ideas between Labour and the Liberal Democrats of the kind that has taken place in Scotland; and no wider debate of the kind stimulated by the Scottish Constitutional Convention.

467 There is clearly a risk of a re-run of the 1970s, with Wales being overshadowed by Scotland. The risk may be that much greater if the Wales Bill is introduced in the same parliamentary session as that for Scotland. Wales needs to have its own, separate debate about the design of a Welsh Assembly. To allow time for that debate, and space free from the dominance of Scotland, it might be worth considering postponing the legislation until a later session.

468 It may be felt that Wales would then be taking second place; and that if it misses the first legislative round, there may not be another one. But the risks of precipitate introduction of legislation for a Welsh Assembly could be even greater. Among the lessons of the 1978 debacle are that the electorate needs time to come to terms with a major policy initiative of this kind; that the proposals need to be debated nationally in their own right, and not just as part of a general election campaign; and that opposition may grow if the debate suggests that the scheme is half-baked, or is seen as half-hearted.

469 There may also be a case for holding a referendum, given the strong rejection of the Government's plans in 1979; and for holding a referendum before introducing the legislation, in case the electorate's views have not changed. The main considerations surrounding the holding of a referendum were set out in chapter 12. For the present discussion, another feature of a referendum is that it can contribute significantly to public education on an issue, especially if held in more propitious circumstances than 1979, when the Government was on its last legs. It generates intense media interest and a lot of public information material, taking the debate out from the politicians to the general public.

470 A wider public debate may be needed if a Welsh Assembly is to gain public consent and support. It is not enough that the opposition political parties have developed their positions. So far none has done much to test the water outside the narrows of the party. The Government that takes office will have to develop its position, which may be different once Cabinet colleagues and the Whitehall machine become involved. The Government will have to persuade both Wales and the rest of the country about the proposed Assembly. The public opinion surveys reported in chapter 1 suggest there may not yet be sufficient of a ground swell in its favour - that may take time, with much greater public consultation and discussion than has taken place so far.

The Legislative Timetable

471 In the 1970s the preparation and passage of devolution legislation occupied the whole of a five-year Parliament. It was meant to be a fast track measure, because of the nationalist pressures, and the Government's potential dependence on nationalist support; and the Government's original intention was to introduce the legislation in 1975. Despite this it took two years and nine months from the Government assuming office in February 1974 before the first Scotland and Wales Bill was introduced in November 1976. This was not for lack of resources or Ministerial push: Ted Short was charged by Harold Wilson with co-ordinating and driving the legislation forward, and the Constitution Unit in the Cabinet Office responsible for preparing the Bill had 30-40 high grade staff (the normal size of a bill team being three to five people).

472 What is the timetable likely to be next time? It will depend on the political priority given to the legislation; the links with Scotland; how the legislation is couched; and whether the Government decides to hold a referendum. The political priorities will be the determining factor, but within certain technical constraints. The main constraint within Government will be the time taken by Cabinet colleagues and Whitehall departments to agree the contents of a Welsh devolution bill and the time it takes to draft. If held in advance of the introduction of legislation, a referendum could be a delaying factor, because there would need to be separate legislation to authorise the referendum. The enabling legislation could be introduced in the first session of a new Government, and the referendum could be held within months of the legislation being passed. During that first year the preparation of the main legislation could be put in hand; but the devolution legislation itself could not be introduced until the second year (although if the first session of the new Parliament is a long one, this could still be during the first session).

473 This is illustrated schematically in **Table 15**, which sets out four possible timescales for the key stages in the preparation and implementation of devolution legislation.

474 The first row shows a very fast-track measure, with a bill being introduced in the first year. For realism this should be compared with the actual 1970s timetable reproduced in the fourth row of the table. The time for consultation with Ministerial colleagues and other departments, which in the 1970s took two years, has been telescoped into three to six months; in practice this may mean agreeing the details before entering into Government.

475 The second row shows the possible impact on the timetable of holding a referendum before introducing the main legislation. If the referendum legislation were passed swiftly in the first year the overall timetable might only be delayed by six months or so. The third row shows a

Table 15: Possible Timescale For Preparing and Introducing Legislation

	Year 1				Year 2				Year 3				Year 4	
	Q1	Q2	Q3	Q4	Q1	Q2	Q3	Q4	Q1	Q2	Q3	Q4	Q1	Q2
Fast-track Bill	Negotiate with Cabinet and Whitehall		Publish White Paper; Prepare Draft Bill	Introduce Wales Bill	Parliamentary passage		Royal Assent	Elections	Assembly and Executive take up office					
Fast-track Bill preceded by referendum		Publish White Paper; Introduce Referendum Bill	Draft Wales Bill	Royal Assent for Referendum Bill; Hold referendum	Introduce Wales Bill	Parliamentary passage		Royal Assent for Wales Bill		Elections	Assembly and Executive take up office			
Medium-track Bill	Negotiate with Cabinet and Whitehall						Publish White Paper	Prepare Draft Bill	Introduce Wales Bill	Parliamentary passage		Royal Assent		Elections
1970s Bill replayed		Issue Green Paper	Publish first White Paper	Negotiate with Cabinet and Whitehall			Publish second White Paper	Negotiate with Cabinet and Whitehall			Prepare Draft Bill	Introduce Bill		

timetable which allows more time for consultation within Government, leading to introduction of the devolution legislation in the second year. This was the timetable originally intended by the Government in the 1970s, but which in the event they failed to achieve. The third row also allows more time for implementation; but the timetable after passage of the legislation could be fast-track as in the first row. Finally, the last row shows the actual 1970s timetable, with the first devolution bill planned for October 1975 being eventually introduced in November 1976.

476 One further comment is called for, on the need for a White Paper. If a referendum were held before introduction of the legislation, the Government would need to publish a White Paper setting out its plans for a Welsh Assembly in some detail. The electorate would need a clear set of proposals on which to express a view; as would institutions and organisations of all kinds who would need to decide how their interests were likely to be affected.

477 Even if no referendum is held, there is still a case for publishing a White Paper. A White Paper would provide the basis for wider public debate; and it is a normal and necessary step in the preparation of sound legislation. The report of the Hansard Society Commission on the Legislative Process contains a reminder about the detrimental effects on legislation of excessive haste and inadequate consultation. Its witnesses commended the growing use of consultation documents and other forms of pre-legislative consultation (showing that it can be done, when Government has a mind to); but more frequently they deplored the lack of it. When time permits it is also good practice to publish the draft bill in time for interested organisations to comment. With major constitutional bills like a Welsh devolution bill it could also be good politics: the Government should not be frightened of allowing a public debate to take place.

The Form of the Legislation

478 One reason why the 1970s devolution legislation took so long to prepare was the way in which it was couched. It contained no clear statement of principle as to which powers were to be devolved and which retained; and it was the product of endless bilateral negotiations with the Whitehall departments, seeking to establish which of their powers and functions might be devolved to the new Assembly. Chapter 2 contains a critique of the Wales Act 1978; and there is a similar critique of the Scotland Act 1978 in the Unit's report on *Scotland's Parliament*. The lawyers we have consulted are united in condemning the 1978 legislation as being excessively lengthy and complex.

479 Possible alternatives were discussed in Chapter 5. For an Assembly with **executive powers** only, legislation on the 1978 model would require the same lengthy schedules enumerating the powers to be transferred. Even if they were merely updated to take account of new legislation since 1978 revision of these schedules would take months and possibly upwards of a year to negotiate with all the Whitehall departments. The alternative mentioned in chapter 5 would be to draft the legislation in broad terms, transferring all the executive powers which prior to devolution were exercisable by the Secretary of State for Wales. This would permit less addition to and subtraction from those powers than took place in the 1978 settlement; but it would be a great deal simpler and quicker to draft.

480 If the Assembly has **legislative powers,** then there are alternative models to the 1978 Act which are also discussed in chapter 5. The main alternative proposed there is the Government of Ireland Act 1920 which established the Parliament in Northern Ireland. Instead of defining the

powers devolved it defines the powers retained, which again makes for simpler drafting. The list of reserved matters was relatively short, because Stormont enjoyed a high degree of devolution; but the list could be made longer without destroying the clarity and simplicity of the Government of Ireland Act model.

481   There is thus a potential trade-off between the nature of the devolution settlement and the time it takes to prepare. There may also be trade-offs between the drafting of the legislation and ease of parliamentary passage: Parliament is less likely to agree to devolution legislation being passed in enabling form, leaving most of the detail to secondary legislation.

The Links with Scotland

482   The Labour Party has said that they will introduce legislation for Scotland and Wales in the first year of a new parliament. The stages which would need to be compressed into that first year have been set out above and illustrated in Table 15. For it to be possible to prepare instructions to Parliamentary Counsel within months of assuming office, an incoming Government would need to have reached agreement on all the essential points in the legislation, and much of the detail, and ideally would have a White Paper ready in draft. Political considerations may require the Welsh legislation to follow the same timescale as Scotland; but there are two technical reasons why it might be advisable to wait until the Scottish legislation has gone through.

483   The first is simply pressure of parliamentary time. The Constitution Unit's earlier report, *Delivering Constitutional Reform,* shows that in a typical session the Government introduces 50-60 programme bills for which there are only 400 hours of legislative time on the floor of the House of Commons. In 1977-78 the Scotland Act took up 160 hours of government time on the floor; and the Wales Act 80 hours. Both Bills were guillotined at the outset. If this experience were repeated, two devolution bills between them could take up over 50% of the Government's legislative time. Even if both bills were ready at the same time, the managers of the legislative programme might conclude that one major constitutional bill was enough for one session.

484   There could be advantages for Wales from allowing Scotland to go first. It would enable the Government to take account of the lessons of the Scottish experience in such matters as the division of powers, the electoral system, entrenchment and so on: all the difficult issues considered in this report. It is almost impossible to cross-fertilise (as the bill team found in 1977-78) if the bills are going through Parliament at the same time. A year's delay would enable Wales genuinely to benefit from the Scottish experience, and to depart from the Scottish model where it seemed right for Wales to do so.

Parliamentary Procedures

485   The convention is that 'first class constitutional measures' take their committee stage on the floor of the House of Commons. It would certainly not be possible to refer the committee stage of a Welsh Assembly bill to a standing committee of Welsh MPs, because the bill would have implications which go much wider than Wales. But it might be possible to relax the convention that the whole of the committee stage of a first class constitutional measure must be taken on the floor. This possibility was explored in the Unit's report, *Delivering Constitutional Reform,* which identified three possible ways of easing the passage of constitutional measures:

- partial referral of the committee stage to standing committee.
- advance timetabling for all bills.
- carry-over of selective bills to the next session.

486 With partial referral of the committee stage to standing committee, the key clauses would still be taken on the floor of the House of Commons, and the detail of the bill would be debated in committee upstairs. This is the procedure followed with the Finance Bill, which used to be taken entirely on the floor; it is a procedure which could also be applied to constitutional bills. The other two changes are about the more effective management of parliamentary time. Automatic timetabling has been recommended in more than one report of the Select Committee on Procedure. It would lead to negotiation of an agreed timetable at the outset for all stages of a bill, rather than the Government seeking to impose a guillotine half way through. Limited carry-over of certain bills would be a more significant departure from existing practice, but it is used in some other Westminster systems and could be experimented with selectively in the UK.

The Implementation Timetable

The First Elections

487 Chapter 11 considered possible electoral systems for the Welsh Assembly: 'first past the post'; single transferable vote; or the additional member system. If a proportional representation system is chosen, both the officials supervising the elections and the parties fighting them would need time to prepare to conduct an election under a different system; and the time may vary depending upon the system chosen. On the official side, the elections will be organised by local returning officers in the usual way: supervised either by the Welsh Office, as in the case of the 1979 referendum, or by the Home Office, as in the case of parliamentary, European and local government elections.

488 The elections cannot of course be held until the devolution legislation has received Royal Assent. Assuming Royal Assent in July of the second year of a new Government (see Table 15), elections could be held in October if the election is by 'first past the post', or in the following spring if it is by proportional representation. The returning officers will require training for a new system, which for STV could be supplied by officials in Northern Ireland; and for AMS by visits to Germany. That should only take a matter of weeks. A longer lead-in time is likely to be needed by the political parties, who for STV will need to prepare a balanced range of candidates in multi-member constituencies, and for AMS will need to draw up regional or national party lists. They will need to decide whether MPs and councillors should be allowed to stand; whether their selection procedures need adaptation to select multiple candidates or to draw up ordered lists (some might want to hold primaries); and if German law were followed, only parties recognised by the state would be allowed to present party lists. All this suggests that six to nine months might be necessary to enable the parties to prepare themselves; but they could start preparing before Royal Assent.

Administrative Preparation and Shadow Running

489 From the point of Royal Assent, preparatory work could be undertaken by the Welsh Office in finding a suitable building, recruiting key staff, etc. In the recent local government reorganisation the lead-in time from Royal Assent to the new local authorities 'going live' was 21 months (July 1994 to April 1996). Of that time, 11 months was a shadow period after the new authorities had been elected before they assumed their responsibilities. That however involved 22 unitary authorities taking over from eight county and 37 district councils. The devolved Government, on the other hand, would largely involve a take-over of one from one, with the new Welsh Executive taking over the existing Welsh Office from the Secretary of State. There should be a lot more that the Secretary of State could set in hand in anticipation of the needs of the Executive, so that once the elections were held the Executive could assume office almost immediately.

490 The Assembly will also require some advance preparation by the Secretary of State. A chief executive will need to be appointed (perhaps in consultation with the other party leaders in Wales); and he or she can then proceed to appoint the staff. The Assembly will need to adopt its own language policy; since all the opposition parties are committed to a fully bilingual Assembly there is likely to be a need for most senior staff to be bilingual. Once the Assembly is elected it may need three to six months to work out standing orders and the other procedures and systems that it intends to use. The Assembly can elect an Executive straight away; but for the first few months the Executive will not be fully accountable to the Assembly, while the Assembly is establishing its procedures.

Accommodation

491 Whichever building is chosen, work will be needed to make it suitable for the Assembly and its staff. A chamber for plenary sessions will have to be created, together with committee rooms, facilities for the media, and office accommodation for the Assembly members and staff. But the preparation of the building need not delay the inauguration of the new Assembly: the new Parliament in Northern Ireland operated in temporary accommodation for several years in the 1920s before it moved into the Parliament buildings at Stormont.

Staffing

492 There are two issues to consider here: how many staff the new Welsh administration will need; and how they are to be recruited. In the 1970s it was assumed that there would need to be an increase in staff of almost 50%; and that all the Welsh Office staff would automatically transfer across. Neither assumption necessarily holds true in the 1990s. Public expenditure constraints are tighter; and with privatisation, contracting out and Next Steps executive agencies, more civil service work is put out to contract, leading to a need for different skills and experience within the core civil service.

493 The Welsh Office has been part of these changes. It provides relatively few services direct, but relies on other bodies - local authorities, the health service and its own executive quangos - to deliver services within the policy and resources framework which it lays down. It has created

only two Next Steps executive agencies (CADW and the Welsh Planning Inspectorate), but the Highways Directorate could be another candidate, and it has already been given greater operational freedom along Next Steps lines. Increasing amounts of work are contracted out to the private sector (e.g. legal work and architects' and surveyors' services), and the process of contracting out is set to continue under the present Government. The Welsh Office itself has been restructured on more business orientated lines following a senior management review in March 1995. It is only possible to speculate about what an incoming Government might do about these developments. They might not be continued, and might to an extent be reversed. And even if they continued in Whitehall it is possible that a devolved administration might wish to conduct things differently in Wales.

494 In any event, it seems likely that the devolved Government would wish to have the core functions of policy advice and administration undertaken by its own staff. It might wish to start afresh in terms of recruitment; but it takes time and it is expensive to make existing staff redundant and start anew. Reasons of speed and economy may decide the new administration to continue with the existing Welsh Office staff; and reasons of practicality suggest that they may not wish to lose the knowledge, skills and experience that exists in the present Welsh Office. As for the size of the staff required for the new administration and Assembly, there will be intense conflicting pressures. Following the Chancellor's latest Budget (November 1995), the Welsh Office is set to reduce from 2,500 staff in 1994-95 to 2,100 in 1996-97. The existing structures may feel stretched to the limit and incapable of taking on new functions; but there will be very tight budgetary pressures to keep additional costs down to a minimum.

495 What will the additional functions be? There are half a dozen factors which will lead to increased staffing requirements. These factors will apply whether the local government model is adopted, with an Executive Committee present in the Assembly, or whether there is an Executive separate from the Assembly:

- **the Assembly:** the Assembly will require clerks and legal advisers, librarians, official reporters, translators and interpreters and (if separate offices are established) a Welsh Comptroller and Auditor General and staff, and a Welsh Ombudsman.
- **the Welsh Executive:** the Welsh Office has three Ministers; the new Welsh Executive is likely to have seven or eight. Each will need a private office with the usual support staff.
- **the split with the Secretary of State:** a small minority of Welsh Office staff will remain with the Secretary of State to advise on the residual responsibilities. This 'rump' Welsh Office will diminish over time; but the split will create a small permanent staffing increase.
- **demands of the Assembly:** increased accountability will create a need for additional resources. At present, oral Questions to Welsh Office Ministers occur once every three weeks. There is one Welsh Day debate a year, and one Select Committee on Welsh Affairs. Against that, although the Welsh Assembly may not be in permanent session, it is likely to sit at least half the year; it is likely to have half a dozen subject committees, which will all generate work for the administration; and oral questions and plenary session debates will occur weekly if not daily. All this will mean a considerable increase in workload for the staff of the Welsh Executive.
- **demands of co-ordinating and consultative machinery:** this report has identified the need for additional co-ordinating machinery if the Welsh administration is to work effectively with local government, Whitehall and the institutions of the EU. This also means an increase in workload, particularly at senior levels.

- **independence from Whitehall:** the Welsh Office relies on Whitehall for a large number of common services (the Treasury; Parliamentary Counsel; Treasury Solicitors; the Central Statistical Office, HMSO, etc). The new Welsh administration will have to be more self-sufficient, and either establish similar services or buy them in on an agency basis.
- **public expectations:** the Welsh people and organisations in the public and private sector will expect an increased standard of service as a result of devolution, with different policies for Wales, and a more responsive administration generally. It is impossible to quantify, but this factor is likely to create the greatest pressure for staff increases.

The Costs of Implementation

496 Increased staff costs are the main item in estimating the increase in costs resulting from devolution; and the main reason for the variation between the various estimates which have been made. None of the political parties which proposes an Assembly has published any costings, but Conservative Secretaries of State have produced estimates; the Cardiff Business School has done a study for BBC Wales; and there are the Government's figures from the 1970s, which are set out in Table 16.

Table 16: The Government's Cost Estimates in the 1970s

The Explanatory and Financial Memorandum to the Wales Bill 1977 gave these estimates:

"Financial effects of the Bill

The Bill will involve increases in accommodation and staff costs. These arise partly from entirely new activities, partly from loss of economies of scale in support of services and partly from divisions of responsibility between Westminster and the new devolved administration. The estimates of additional costs relate to the organisation and levels of service as they are expected to be when the new administration takes over its responsibilities in the devolved fields. The numbers of additional staff expected to be required are referred to under the public service manpower heading.

Capital expenditure will be incurred to establish the Welsh Assembly and it is estimated to comprise (at November 1977 prices):

(i) about £3 million on the adaptation and equipment of the Exchange in Cardiff for the use of the Assembly;

(ii) about £1 million on the provision and equipment of office accommodation arising from the creation of the Assembly and the consequent reorganisation of the Welsh Office.

Additional annual running costs, from the take-over of responsibilities, are broadly assessed as follows (at November 1977 prices):

(iii) about £3 million in respect of salaries and related costs of members of the Welsh Assembly and in respect of services for the Assembly;

(iv) about £9½ million in respect of additional civil servants in Wales, including staff of the Welsh Comptroller and Auditor General and related costs, including accommodation costs.

The costs of the referendum, the initial elections and the attendant publicity on both referendum and elections are estimated broadly at £1¼ million. There will also be expenditure of about £1¼ million in respect of the initial removal of staff to Cardiff.

Effects of the Bill on Public Service Manpower

The number of civil servants in Wales is likely to increase by about 1,150 over forecast levels. This figure includes staff to support the Welsh Comptroller and Auditor General."

497 In today's prices the Government's estimate of capital expenditure would be around £14m; the annual running costs of the Assembly would be £10m, and of the additional civil servants £33m. It is useful to break the figures down under these three headings when comparing the different cost estimates which follow.

Table 17: Capital and Running Costs of a Welsh Assembly

Estimate	Initial Capital Cost £m	Assembly Annual Running Costs £m	Additional Civil Servants Annual Cost £m
Labour Government 1977 (uprated to current prices)	14	10	33
Cardiff Business School 1996[66]	10	13	-
William Hague 1996[67]	24	17	11
John Redwood 1995[68]	13	25	19 (staff) 67 (new policies)

498 A number of points should be noted about these different estimates:
- the figures are only roughly comparable, because with some estimates it is not clear exactly what is being counted. The study by the Cardiff Business School is the most detailed, but looks only at the direct costs of the Assembly.
- the estimates assume that members of the Assembly will be full-time. The Business School estimate the annual salaries and expenses of 100 full-time members at £7.5m. If (as noted in Chapter 6) membership of the Assembly might be part-time, then members' salaries might reduce pro rata.
- the table omits the cost of Assembly elections. The Business School estimate this at £0.85m per annum, annualising over a four-year term the £3.4m estimated cost of the 1992 general election in Wales.
- the main difference between the various estimates is the additional costs falling on the Welsh administration (the final column in Table 17).

499 This last item is the hardest to quantify. All estimates of additional staff costs must be 'guesstimates' because no one knows how many additional staff the new Welsh administration will need or can afford. All it is possible to say is that some additional staff will be required, on top of the staff working directly for the Assembly, for the reasons set out in paragraph 495. For every 100 additional civil servants required the annual cost (including all overheads) is around £3m. This figure is derived from the annual running costs of the Welsh Office: its budget for 1995-96 is £6.77bn, of which 1.2% (£76m) was devoted to the running costs of 2,500 staff.

Conclusion

500 The timetable for introducing devolution legislation to Wales will depend on the political priority attached to it; the links with Scotland; the way the legislation is framed; whether there is a referendum; and whether the Government is willing to allow time for a separate debate in Wales. In the 1970s it took nearly three years to prepare the first Scotland and Wales Bill.

501 The first elections to a Welsh Assembly could be held within three months of the legislation receiving Royal Assent if conducted under 'first past the post', or nine months if by a proportional representation system, to allow the political parties time to prepare. If the legislation is introduced in the second year of a new Government the Welsh Assembly could be elected and the Welsh Executive take up office towards the end of the third year. A referendum would require enabling legislation and would prevent the devolution legislation being introduced until the second year. The ability of a Government to introduce legislation faster than that will depend upon the time taken by Cabinet colleagues and Whitehall departments to agree the contents of a Welsh devolution bill, and the time it takes to draft.

502 Additional staff will be required for the Assembly itself; to service the Executive Members; to manage the split with the Secretary of State, and greater separation from Whitehall; to respond to additional demands from the Assembly; and the greater expectations of the public. It is not possible to quantify how many additional staff would be required; in the 1970s the estimate was 1,150. Every 100 additional staff of the **Welsh administration** will cost around £3m. The annual running costs of the **Assembly** have been estimated at around £15m.

503 The additional costs of a Welsh Assembly can be considered under four heads: initial capital costs (estimates range from £10m to £24m); direct running costs of the Assembly (£10m to £25m per annum); additional staff costs of the Welsh administration (£11m to £33m per annum); and the cost of Assembly elections (£1m per annum).

Chapter 14

Concluding Observations

Introduction

504 The focus of this report has been on the implementation questions which must be addressed in planning for the introduction of a Welsh Assembly. The report has aimed to identify all the main design features which a new Government will have to decide, and to bring out the technical and the practical issues which must be faced. We have tried to avoid straying too much into political territory; but this emphasis on the technical and practical cannot wholly exclude matters political. The Assembly will be a political institution which will operate in a highly political context, and it will require political skills of a high order to bring the Assembly into being and to ensure that it earns its place amongst Welsh institutions. This final chapter contains some brief observations about the wider political process.

The Wider Political Context

505 First, there will be need for a new kind of politics to make the settlement work; for a new political maturity and tolerance in London, but also in Wales. It is a weakness that there has not been a process in Wales like the Scottish Constitutional Convention, to bring the opposition parties together and enable them to develop a common vision of how the Assembly should operate. It means there has been little public debate, as each party has developed its own private position; and little experience of the processes of discussion, consensus and compromise which can bring political rivals together in support of a common position. It will require imaginative leadership and an outward looking approach amongst the political parties in Wales if the Assembly is to enjoy popular and cross-party support.

506 This will not be easy in a country where there is still mistrust between North and South, between English and Welsh speakers, and between Labour and the other parties. An Assembly could be a major unifying institution in Wales; but it will require a minimum degree of unity to bring it about. The parties' failure in 1979 to join together in a common cause during the referendum is not an encouraging precedent.

507 Once created the Assembly will evolve as a political institution which will develop a legitimacy and dynamic of its own. There may be many who are disappointed with aspects of the original design; but they should have plenty of opportunities to improve upon it later. The devolution settlement will be continually evolving and adjusting at the margins, in response to shifts in the political, budgetary and other pressures operating in London and Cardiff. It has rightly been said that devolution is a process and not an event. The devolution settlement enshrined in the Government of Ireland Act 1920 was subject to continuous minor adjustment in subsequent Acts of the Westminster Parliament. It will be the same in Wales. The Wales Act will be the start of the devolution process, but not necessarily its conclusion.

508 The devolution settlement will also need to adjust in line with shifts in the wider decentralisation of power within the UK. The Welsh Assembly is unlikely to be legislated for on its own, but as part of a wider process of devolution involving legislation for a Scottish Parliament, and some measure of greater decentralisation to the English regions. This programme of asymmetrical, rolling devolution will require imagination and flexibility if it is to be carried through; but other European countries show that it can be done.

509 Through her contacts with other European regions Wales has seen at first hand how France, Italy and Spain have all developed regional self-government in recent years, and accommodated surprising degrees of diversity in each case.[69]   They show that the transition from a centralised, unitary state to a decentralised and more diversified model is possible, without threatening the unity of the state or adding to the pressures for separatism. The process will not be easy, will raise many difficult issues (not least over finance), and will require adjustments by the political parties and all the institutions of the British state. How the central government machine might need to change under devolution, and the machinery of government implications of other constitutional reforms are themes to be explored by the Constitution Unit in a further publication later in 1996.

Appendix A

Executive Bodies

Name of Body	Annual Expenditure (93/94) £m	Number of Staff April 1994	Time Commitment & Salary - Chair	Number Time Commitment & Salary - Members	Specialist Expertise	Greater Impetus and Dynamism	Operational and Financial Freedom	Public/ Private Sector Partnerships	Cultural Freedom	Professional Independence	Comments
1 Agriculture Wages Committees (AWC)	0.002		4 meetings per annum £86 per meeting	12 4 meetings per annum £100 per meeting	•••					•••	Industry specific. Non-political.
2 Arts Council of Wales	13.9		2 days per week £nil	16 18 days per annum	•••		•	•	•••		Specialist expertise. Need to support innovation and 'unpopular' art.
3 Cardiff Bay Development Corporation	47.55	88	Chair – 2.5 days per week £33700 pa Deputy – 2 days per week £19010 pa	12 0.5 days per week £5375 pa	••	•••	••	•••			Commercial freedom. Return to local government in due course.
4 Countryside Council for Wales	19.88	337	Chair – 2.5 days per week £30855 pa Deputy – 5 days per month £13300 pa	8 2.5 days per month £6650 pa	••	•	•				Scientific expertise. Representation of competing countryside interests.
5 Curriculum and Assessment Authority for Wales	1.74	25	Chair – 2 days per week £21905 pa Deputy – 2 days per month £5265 pa	13 1 day per month £nil	•••				•	•	Specialist expertise.

Name of Body	Annual Expenditure (93/94) £m	Number of Staff April 1994	Time Commitment & Salary - Chair	Number Time Commitment & Salary - Members	Specialist Expertise	Greater Impetus and Dynamism	Operational and Financial Freedom	Public/Private Sector Partnerships	Cultural Freedom	Professional Independence	Comments
6 Development Board for Rural Wales	24.9	120	Chair - 2 days per week £36610 pa	10 2 days per month £36610 pa	●●	●●●	●●	●●●			Could be devolved to local government or merged with WDA
7 Further Education Funding Council for Wales	143.14	34	Chair - 1 day per week £10425 pa Deputy £ ex officio	11 1.5 days per month £2255 pa	●●	●				●	Resource allocation function.
8 Higher Education Funding Council for Wales	178.98	27	Chair - 4 days per month £11270 pa Deputy £ ex officio	10 1.5 days per month £2255 pa	●●	●			●	●	Tradition of arms length funding to preserve universities' independence.
9 Housing for Wales	161.16	75	Chair - 2.5 days per week £30710 pa Deputy - 1.5 days per week £14275 pa	5 3 days per month £6255 pa	●●		●●	●			Could transfer to local government.
10 Land Authority for Wales	12.3	45	Chair - 2.5 days per week £32495 pa Deputy - 1 day per week £9230 pa	7 3.5 days per month £6490 pa	●●●	●●●	●●●	●●●			Self-financing. Commercial success.

Name of Body	Annual Expenditure (93/94) £m	Number of Staff April 1994	Time Commitment & Salary - Chair	Number Time Commitment & Salary - Members	Specialist Expertise	Greater Impetus and Dynamism	Operational and Financial Freedom	Public/Private Sector Partnerships	Cultural Freedom	Professional Independence	Comments
11 National Library of Wales	6.52	170		52 6 days per annum £nil	••	•	•	•	•••		Specialist expertise. Independent acquisitions policy.
12 National Museum of Wales	16.8	382.5		40 4 days per annum £nil	••	•	•	•	•••		Specialist expertise. Independent acquisitions policy.
13 Royal Commission on Ancient & Historical Monuments in Wales	1.213	34.5		10	•••				••	•	Specialist expertise.
14 Sports Council for Wales	8.63	172	Chair - 2 days per week £16375 pa Deputy - 1.5 days per week £8910 pa	12 1 day per month £nil	••	•	•		•		Specialist expertise.
15 Wales Tourist Board	13.81	107.5	Chair - 3 days per week £33625 pa	6 2 days per month £6650	••	•••		••			Specialist expertise.
16 Wales Youth Agency	0.40	10.5	Chair - 12-15 days pa £2500 pa Deputy - 12-15 days pa £2500 pa	11 4-5 days per annum £nil	••	•					Consider for abolition or transfer to local government

Name of Body	Annual Expenditure (93/94) £m	Number of Staff April 1994	Time Commitment & Salary - Chair	Number Time Commitment & Salary - Members	Specialist Expertise	Greater Impetus and Dynamism	Operational and Financial Freedom	Public/ Private Sector Partnerships	Cultural Freedom	Professional Independence	Comments
17 Welsh Development Agency (WDA)	151.66	443	Chair – 2 days per week £36610 pa	7 1 member @ £10060 pa 3 days per month 5 @ £6705 pa 2 days per month	●●	●●●	●●	●●●			Specialist expertise. Partnership with private sector. Operational freedom.
18 Welsh Language Board (WLB)	0.13	8	Chair –2 days per week £21640 pa	14 2 days per month £5265 pa	●●	●			●●●		Emotive issue. Keep at arms length from politics.
19 Welsh National Board for Nursing Midwifery and Health Visiting	1.27	27.5	Chair – 2 days per week £9684 pa	6 2 days per month £nil	●●●					●●	Specialist expertise.

Source for cols 1-5: Cabinet Office, Public Bodies 1994

Column 2 gives the annual expenditure of each body. In some cases this is greater than its government grant, because it raises money through trading or from other sources.

Columns 4 and 5 show the time commitment of the chairmen and board members, and where paid the level of salary. Most of the chairmen are paid; but in just under half of the executive quangos the board members are unpaid.

The next six columns score each of the quangos according to the criteria set out in chapter 8 under the heading 'reasons for maintaining independent quangos'. ●●● indicate that particular reason strongly applies; a blank suggests it does not apply at all. The final column records in most cases the main reason for the body requiring a degree of independence. In some cases it suggests an alternative line of accountability or control e.g. transfer to local government.

Appointments by the Secretary of State

APPOINTMENTS BY THE SECRETARY OF STATE FOR WALES

Advisory Committee on Borderline Substances
Advisory Committee on Pesticides
Agricultural Wages Board for England and Wales
Agricultural Wages Committees x 6
Agriculture Advisory Panel for Wales
Art for Architecture Awards Panel
Arts Council of Wales
Audit Commission
Boundary Commission for Wales
British Pharmacopoeia Commission
British Wool Marketing Board
Building Regulations Advisory Committee
Cardiff Bay Development Corporation
Committee of Investigation for Great Britain
Committee on Agricultural Valuation Wales
Committee on Safety of Medicines
Community Health Councils x 22
Consultative Panel on Badgers and Bovine Tuberculosis
Consumers Committee for Great Britain
Council of St. David's University, Lampeter
Countryside Council for Wales
Court and Council of University College of Wales, Aberystwyth
Court of Cranfield Institute of Technology
Court of University College of North Wales, Bangor
Court of University College, Swansea
Curriculum and Assessment Authority for Wales
Dental Auxiliaries Committee
Dental Practice Board
Development Board for Rural Wales
District Health Authorities x 8
Environment Agency
Family Health Service Authorities x 8
Farm Animal Welfare Council
Food from Britain Council
Forestry Commission Reference/Committee Panel (Wales)
Further Education Funding Council for Wales
Health Promotion Authority for Wales
Higher Education Funding Council for Wales
Hill Farming Advisory Committee for England, Wales and Northern Ireland
Hill Farming Advisory Committee for England, Wales and Northern Ireland-
    Sub Committee for Wales
Historic Buildings Committee for Wales
Home Grown Cereals Authority
Housing for Wales
Human Fertilisation and Embryology Authority
Independent Appeals Authority for School Examinations

Intervention Board for Agricultural Produce
Joint Committee on Vaccination and Immunisation
Joint Nature Conservation Committee
Land Authority for Wales
Library and Information Services Council (Wales)
Local Government Boundary Commission for Wales
Meat and Livestock Commission
Meat and Livestock Commission Consumers Committee
Medical Officer for Complaints
Medical Practices Committee
Medicines Commission
Mental Handicap Advisory Panel
Mental Health Act Commission
Milk Development Council
National Advisory Council for Education and Training Targets
National Institute of Agricultural Botany Council
National Library of Wales, Council
National Library of Wales, Court of Governors
National Museum of Wales, Council
National Museum of Wales, Court of Governors
National Parks Committee x 3
National Radiological Protection Board
National Rivers Authority
National Rivers Authority Advisory Committee for Wales
National Rivers Authority Regional Flood Defence Committee
NHS Trusts x 29
Office of Water Services
Place Names Advisory Committee
Plant Variety and Seeds Tribunal
Potato Marketing Board
Public Health Laboratory Service Board
Radioactive Waste Management Advisory Committee
Rent Assessment Panel for Wales
Residuary Body for Wales
Residuary Milk Marketing Board
Salmon Advisory Committee
Saundersfoot Harbour Commission
Sea Fish Industry Authority
Sea Fisheries Industry Authority
Sea Fisheries Committee : North Western and North Wales
Sea Fisheries Committee : South Wales
Sports Council for Wales
Sportsmatch Awards panel
Staff Commission for Wales
Standing Dental Advisory Committee
Standing Medical Advisory Committee
Standing Nursing and Midwifery Advisory Committee
Standing Pharmaceutical Advisory Committee

United Kingdom Central Council for Nursing, Midwifery and Health Visiting
Urban Investment Grant Appraisal panel
Wales Tourist Board
Wales Youth Agency
Welsh Committee for Postgraduate Pharmaceutical Education
Welsh Council for Postgraduate Medical and Dental Education
Welsh Development Agency
Welsh Economic Council
Welsh Health Common Services Authority
Welsh Industrial Development Advisory Board
Welsh Language Board
Welsh National Board for Nursing, Midwifery and Health Visiting
Welsh Scheme for the Development of Health and Social Research

Source: Welsh Office, *Appointments by the Secretary of State for Wales*, September 1995.

Glossary

This report suggests that if an Assembly is created in Wales there could be a separate Executive answerable to the Assembly and carrying out most of the functions currently performed by the Welsh Office. This creates the need for terminology to distinguish the functions of the Assembly and the Executive, and in this report the following terms are used:

Welsh Assembly or Senedd	The new Welsh Assembly, which might have limited legislative powers; powers of democratic control and scrutiny; but no executive power. The body could, if desired, be called the Senedd or the Welsh Parliament.
Members of the Welsh Assembly (MWA)	All the members of the Welsh Assembly, who wouldcomprise:

	Executive Members	those members with executive (Ministerial) portfolios
	Backbenchers	those members (the majority) without portfolios.

Welsh Executive or Welsh Government	The group of Executive Members, chosen from and answerable to the Assembly, carrying out the responsibilities of devolved government in Wales. They could, if desired, be called Welsh Ministers; collectively they would form the equivalent of a Welsh Cabinet.
Welsh Administration	The body of officials serving the Welsh Executive.
Welsh Office	The existing Welsh Office.
Secretary of State	The existing Secretary of State for Wales; or in future, the Minister in the British Cabinet responsible for Wales and relations with the Welsh Executive

References

1   Vernon Bogdanor, *Devolution,* 1979.

2   *Ibid.*

3   *Ibid.*

4   *Democracy and Devolution: Proposals for Scotland and Wales,* Cmnd 5732, September 1974.

5   Foulkes, Jones and Wilford eds., *The Welsh Veto,* 1983.

6   *Wales: The Challenge and the Record,* March 1994.

7   Rt Hon Tony Blair MP, *Speech to Labour Party Conference,* 3 October 1995.

8   Foulkes, Jones and Wilford eds., *The Welsh Veto,* 1983.

9   *South Wales Echo,* 21 February 1979.

10   Nicholas Edwards, *Western Mail,* 2 February 1979.

11   Boyne, Griffiths et al, *Local Government in Wales,* 1991.

12   Welsh Office, *Welsh Local Government Financial Statistics No 18,* 1994.

13   *Ibid.*

14   All figures supplied by Cardiff Business School.

15   Kevin Morgan & Ellis Roberts, *The Democratic Deficit - A Guide to Quangoland,* 1993.

16   John Mackintosh, *The Devolution of Power,* 1968; *Report of the Royal Commission on the Constitution,* Cmnd 5460, 1973; Vernon Bogdanor, *Devolution,* 1979; John Osmond ed., *A Parliament for Wales,* 1994.

17   John Osmond, *A Parliament for Wales,* 1994.

18   Ron Davies, *Speech on the Regeneration of the Valleys to a Rhondda Conference,* November 1992.

19   Professor Kevin Morgan, 'Development from within - economic renewal and a Welsh parliament' in *A Parliament for Wales,* 1994.

20   Barry Jones, 'Welsh Politics come of Age' in John Osmond ed., *A Parliament for Wales,* 1994.

21   John Osmond ed., *A Parliament for Wales,* 1994.

22   John Hopkins, *Regional Government in Europe,* unpublished research paper prepared for the Constitution Unit.

23   Stanley de Smith and Rodney Brazier, *Constitutional and Administrative Law,* 7th edition 1994.

24   Welsh Labour Action is a group within the Wales Labour Party pressing for an Assembly with legislative power and elected by proportional representation, as reported in *Western Mail,* 27 September 1995.

25   Harry Calvert, *Constitutional Law of Northern Ireland,* 1968.

26   As for example in the Malaysian Constitution, Article 76A.

27   Rt Hon Tony Blair MP, *John Smith Memorial Lecture,* 7 February 1996.

28   *Frameworks for the Future,* Cm 2964, September 1995.

29   We are indebted to Nicholas Neal (former Solicitor to South Glamorgan County Council) for preparing this model, by taking the functions of the Welsh Office and superimposing upon them a local government committee structure.

30   Maud Committee on the Management of Local Government (1964-66); Bains Working Group on New Local Authorities Management and Structures (1972); Widdicombe Committee of Enquiry into the Conduct of Local Authority Business (1986). Conclusions summarised in Department of the Environment: *Community Leadership and Representation: Unlocking the Potential,* 1993.

31   'Taking Charge: the Rebirth of Local Democracy', *Municipal Journal,* 1995.

32   *Democracy and Devolution: Proposals for Scotland and Wales,* Cmnd 5732, September 1974.

33 Table 7 shows the Welsh Office organisational chart (February 1996) with six ministerial portfolios superimposed. It is only fair to point out that the cabinet model also uses committees, but mainly staffed by officials.

34 Bernard Crick & David Millar, *To Make the Parliament of Scotland a Model for Democracy*, 1995.

35 *Democracy and Devolution: Proposals for Scotland and Wales* Cmnd 5732, September 1974.

36 The analysis derives from the late John Mackintosh, 'The power of the Secretary of State' in *New Edinburgh Review* no. 31 February 1976. He listed six functions; in this report the last two functions have been combined.

37 In Order 9 of their draft Standing Orders for a Scottish Parliament, *To Make the Parliament of Scotland a Model for Democracy*, 1995.

38 The dismissal of the Australian Prime Minister Gough Whitlam by the Governor General in 1975, and the dismissal of Premier Lang of New South Wales in the 1930s.

39 House of Commons, *Official Report*, HC deb vol 936 col 316, 26 July 1977.

40 I McLean, 'Are Scotland and Wales over-represented in the House of Commons?', *Political Quarterly*, October-December 1995.

41 Ferdinand Mount, *The British Constitution Now*, 1993.

42 Tam Dalyell, *Devolution: the End of Britain*, 1977.

43 Constitution Unit, *Delivering Constitutional Reform*, April 1996. David Butler, 'Modifying Electoral Arrangements,' in David Butler and H.M. Halsey eds., *Policy and Politics* 1978.

44 *The Civil Service: Continuity and Change*, Cm 2627, July 1994.

45 Stuart Weir and Wendy Hall eds., *Ego Trip - Extra-governmental Organisations in the United Kingdom and their Accountability*, Democratic Audit 1994; John Plummer, *The Governance Gap - Quangos and Accountability*, 1994; Alan Greer and Paul Hoggett, 'Non-elected Bodies and Local Governance', in *Commission for Local Democracy Research Report no. 10*, February 1995; Parliamentary Affairs (special issue on Quangos), Spring 1995.

46 Welsh Office, *Appointments by the Secretary of State for Wales*, September 1995.

47 *First Report of the Committee on Standards in Public Life*, Cm 2850-I, 1995.

48 N Rao and K Young, *Local Authority Experience of Compulsory Competitive Tendering*, August 1995.

49 G A Boyne, P Griffiths, A Lawton & J Law, *Local Government in Wales, its Role and Functions*, 1991.

50 HM Treasury, *Needs Assessment Study: Report*, December 1979.

51 Scottish Constitutional Convention, *Scotland's Parliament. Scotland's Right* , November 1995.

52 Patrick Dunleavy, Helen Margetts and Stuart Weir, 'Replaying the Election', *Parliamentary Affairs*, October 1992.

53 Scottish Constitutional Convention, *Towards Scotland's Parliament*, 1990.

54 *Report of the Royal Commission on the Constitution*, Cmnd 5460, 1973.

55 Vernon Bogdanor, *The People and the Party System*, 1981.

56 Scottish Constitutional Convention, *Towards Scotland's Parliament*, 1990.

57 *Ibid.*

58 We are grateful to Paul Wilder of the Arthur McDougall Fund (an independent charity specialising in political science and electoral systems) for devising this scheme, with advice from Tom Ellis (the Fund's Chairman) and John Osmond of the Parliament for Wales Campaign.

59 Cited by Tom Ellis in 'Democracy in Germany: A President Speaks', *Representation* vol 33 no 1, 1995.

60 Peter Hain, *Proportional Mis-representation: the case against PR in Britain*, 1986.

61 Eckhard Jesse, 'The Method of Electing the German Bundestag and its Effect on the Parties', *Representation* vol 33 no 1, 1995.

62 Vernon Bogdanor *The People and the Party System*, 1981.

63   C Munro, 'The Union of 1707 and the British Constitution', in *Scotland and the Union,* Hume Papers on Public Policy vol 2 no 2, Summer 1994.

64   Scottish Constitutional Convention, *Scotland's Parliament. Scotland's Right* , November 1995.

65   The Labour Party, *A Choice for England,* July 1995.

66   Jane Bryan and Stephen Hill, *The Estimated Costs of a Welsh Assembly,* January 1996.

67   *Western Mail,* 29 February 1996.

68   *Conservative Party News,* 16 June 1995.

69   John Hopkins, 'Regional Government in Western Europe' in Stephen Tindale ed., T*he State and the Nations,* 1996; John Hopkins, *Regional Government in Europe,* unpublished research paper prepared for the Constitution Unit.